BIGAMY,
BANKRUPTCY,
WAR AND DIVORCE

BIGAMY, BANKRUPTCY, WAR AND DIVORCE

THE TANGLED LIFE OF A TODDINGTON LANDLADY

RICHARD HART & PAUL BROWN

The History Press

First published 2019

The History Press
97 St George's Place, Cheltenham,
Gloucestershire, GL50 3QB
www.thehistorypress.co.uk

British Library Cataloguing in Publication Data.
A catalogue record for this book is available from the British Library.

ISBN 978 0 7509 9145 2

Typesetting and origination by The History Press
Printed and bound in Great Britain by TJ International Ltd.

CONTENTS

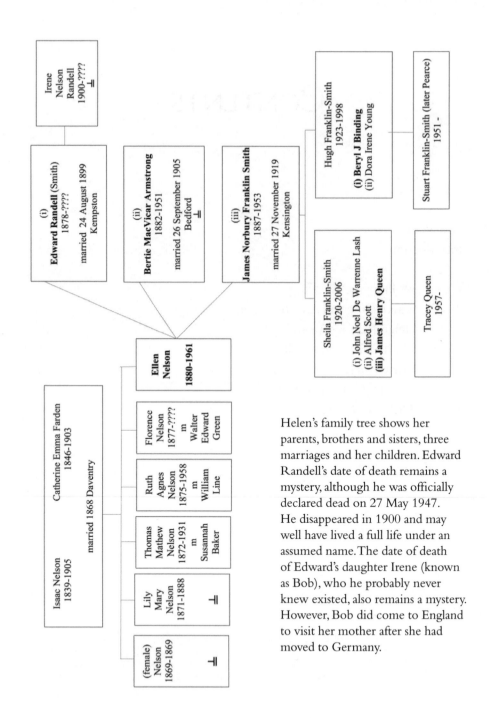

Helen's family tree shows her parents, brothers and sisters, three marriages and her children. Edward Randell's date of death remains a mystery, although he was officially declared dead on 27 May 1947. He disappeared in 1900 and may well have lived a full life under an assumed name. The date of death of Edward's daughter Irene (known as Bob), who he probably never knew existed, also remains a mystery. However, Bob did come to England to visit her mother after she had moved to Germany.

ᖴOREWORD

The love letters of a Toddington landlady only survived because a bank inspector could not bear to throw them away. He found them in a box in a safe in the 1970s, where they had been since they were deposited some time during the First World War. The branch had lost touch with the depositor and so the inspector took the letters home, making notes from the contents with a view to tracking down the owner. He was unsuccessful and they remained in his loft for nearly forty years until he read the book on the history of Lloyds published on the bank's 250th anniversary, and noticed that the author, Richard Hart, came from Toddington. He had found a new home for the letters and passed them on.

With the help of modern technology, and the superb abilities and tenacity of researcher Delia Gleave, the story of Helen Nelson has been pieced together. Helen had a full life and enjoyed many adventures before she was consumed by a deep passion for James Norbury Franklin-Smith, following a chance encounter at a Leighton Buzzard horse show. The letters tell the story of their early relationship.

The bank inspector prefers to remain anonymous but we need to thank him and other members of the Leighton Buzzard Archaeological and Historical Society besides Delia who contributed to compiling this book. Chief among them is Jill Jones, who faithfully transcribed the letters, a daunting task. She was surprised and amused at some of Helen's more risqué asides.

We have also had help from Chris Goddard in chasing down military details and obtaining photographs, and the Western Front Association for background on the Salonika campaign. The Dover Society and the Bedfordshire Archives and Record Service have also been helpful in providing material, as has Maureen Brown, the Society's historical research officer.

Lastly, thanks again to Delia, we managed to track down Helen's descendants, Tracey Queen and Stuart Pierce. It is fair to say that they were both astonished and delighted to hear of their grandmother's colourful past and we thank them for their help and encouragement to publish Helen's letters and record her life.

ℐntroduction

A bundle of passionate but unclaimed love letters written a century ago and found in a London bank vault have led to the uncovering of an extraordinary story.

Research has revealed the adventures of a spirited young woman who by the standards of the time, or perhaps any time, behaved scandalously. Yet she managed to avoid disgrace, get her man, and go on to lead a respectable life.

Ellen, or Helen as she (and we) later called herself, Nelson's behaviour appears shocking on paper. Among other misdeeds, she appears to have been bigamously married, twice. Given her circumstances, however, her survival is a triumph of fortitude over betrayal.

Nothing in her background would suggest the colourful life she would later lead. Ellen was a Bedfordshire policeman's daughter. She was born in 1880 in Marston Moretaine where her father, Isaac, was stationed as the local policeman. He originally came from Cumberland but seems to have settled in Bedfordshire, where he held the post of constable in several of the county's villages.

The 1881 census shows that he and Ellen's mother, Catherine, aged 34, already had four children – three daughters and a son – by the time Ellen came along. The two eldest children had been born in nearby Lidlington, where Isaac had previously been stationed.

The King William IV public house at 36 High Street, Kempston, where Helen Nelson grew up. She was 13 when her father Isaac took over the pub. This is one of the oldest buildings in the town and little has changed since Isaac retired from the police force and became a publican in 1893.

Ten years later Isaac had moved on again and he and his family were living at the police house in Ampthill Road, Westoning, but shortly afterwards, at the age of 44, he retired from the police force and became a publican. At the time this was a common career progression for policemen, who were welcomed by magistrates because they were well able to keep order when their customers became rowdy.

In 1893 Isaac became landlord of a flourishing establishment, the King William IV at Kempston, now a suburb of Bedford. The building, which dates from about 1600, had been a public house since about 1830, when the first licensees are recorded. It was quite large and had a quoits court in the garden and a separate building with a billiard table.

Downstairs the pub had a taproom, bar, cellar, smoke room, kitchen, and scullery. Upstairs there was plenty of room for the family, with four bedrooms, a box room and a WC, and outside there was stabling for five horses.

The interior of the King William IV in 2018. Helen's experience in helping her family run such a large and busy establishment came in useful later in life when she took on The Sow and Pigs at Toddington.

In Victorian days better quality public houses were used for all sorts of purposes. Isaac was clearly regarded as a pillar of the community because in August 1893 he was sworn in as a member of the jury at an inquest held at his pub.

Isaac remained landlord of the King William IV and occasionally got a mention in the local papers in cases where customers had to be removed for being drunk and disorderly, but he was always regarded as an upright citizen. This emphasis on law and order must have left a mark on Ellen but none of this is apparent from her later actions. However, she evidently learned a lot about running public houses from her time at the King William IV, which stood her in good stead in later years.

Sometime before August 1899 she met the man who was to become her first husband. How they met is not known, but her wedding 'of more than ordinary interest' was reported in the *Bedfordshire Mercury* of 25 August 1899.

1

A Glittering Wedding

The *Bedfordshire Mercury* reported Helen Nelson's wedding at All Saints' Church at Kempston near Bedford on 24 August 1899. Her husband seemed a major catch. He was 24-year-old Edward Randell, proprietor of the Empire Palace of Varieties at Dover, and the son of Edward Randell, of 25 Mark Lane, London.

The bride, the youngest daughter of Isaac Nelson, was bedecked in pearls and diamonds (a gift of the groom), and the bridal party was dressed in the latest fashion. So admired were the gowns that on the Saturday before the ceremony they had been displayed for the public to look at in the windows of E.P. Rose & Son, a department store at 50 High Street, Bedford.

The church was full and crowds waited outside for a glimpse of the wedding party.

The wedding, conducted at noon, was described as one of the most stylish that had been solemnized at Kempston for a long time, and the newspaper report goes into a lavish description of the outfits, costumes and flowers. There is a long list of guests and gifts, including a description of the jewels given to the bride by the groom. She in turn gave him a silver-mounted hunting crop.

But this grand occasion was not all that it seemed. There was a notable absentee from the ceremony – the bride's father, Isaac. The bride was

Kempston Parish Church, where Helen married Edward Randell. The lane approaching the church was packed with local sightseers for the grand wedding, and the church itself was full.

Helen's first marriage certificate, showing Edward Randell as proprietor of the Empire, Dover, a music hall. Both Edward and Helen lied about their ages. He was 21, she just 19.

instead given away by her older brother, Thomas Nelson. Another oddity was that the best man, named as Percy Stevenson of Birmingham, was 'prevented at the last moment from attending owing to a sudden illness' and was replaced by a local man, Reginald Stratton.

Close examination of the guests listed in the report has failed to find any relation of the groom, even though every seat in the church was taken. Neither of Mr Randell's parents were present at the ceremony. There were some guests which the paper describes as 'from the theatre', who were probably invited by the groom, but the rest seemed to be Helen's friends and relatives.

The absence of the bride's father, and his omission from the list of people who brought gifts for the couple, is both surprising and intriguing. The King William IV pub, at 36 High Street, Kempston, where the wedding breakfast was to be held, was about a mile from All Saints' Church. According to a report of the wedding in the *Dover Express*, the wedding breakfast was provided by a Mr A. Mann (this was Alfred Mann, a cook from Bedford), but even if Isaac had been organising the reception, it seems likely that if he wanted to attend the ceremony he could have done so. There is no record of Isaac being ill, so perhaps his policeman's instinct told him that the groom was not all that he seemed. Nevertheless, because Helen was under 21, he must have given his consent to the match otherwise the wedding could not have taken place. Perhaps this says a lot about the personality of the bride, and Isaac's inability to resist his youngest daughter's strong will to marry.

Adding to this rather odd set of circumstances is that the bride and groom did not attend their own reception. They had their wedding photographs taken, a rather unusual and expensive innovation at the time, and then left for their honeymoon directly from the church. As the paper put it: 'Almost directly the ceremony was over and they had responded to the abundant congratulations the wedding couple were driven to the Bedford L. & N.W. Station and by the 2.48pm train started on their way to Scarborough, where the honeymoon is to be spent.' After the honeymoon they were to go to Dover, where they would set up home.

Despite the absence of the happy couple, sixty people attended the reception held at the bride's home, the King William IV, where Isaac had erected 'a large marquee in the garden'.

The paper reports an extensive list of guests alongside a description of the lavish gifts the couple had received from them in order to set up their new home in style. There is, however, no explanation of the peculiar aspects of the wedding, particularly the absence of the bride's father.

MARRIAGE OF MISS NELSON.

A wedding of more than ordinary interest was celebrated at All Saints' Church just at noon yesterday. The bride was Miss Helen Nelson, youngest daughter of Mr I. Nelson, of Kempston, and the bridegroom, Mr Edward Randell, proprietor of the Empire Palace of Varieties, Dover, and son of Mr Edward Randell, 25, Mark-lane, London. The church had been specially prepared for the celebration and the the chancel beautifully decorated with lilies and palms by Messrs Laxton Bros, Bedford. Some time before the ceremony every available seat was occupied, and crowds had to content themselves with a glimpse of the bridal party on their entrance and exit. The dresses were all of latest modes and finely made (they had drawn hundreds to the windows of Messrs E. P. Rose & Son, Bedford, when on view there last Saturday), and the wedding was certainly one of the most stylish that has been solemnized at Kempston for a long time. The bride's dress and Court train was of cream corded silk, trimmed with pearl passementerie with transparent yokes and sleeves of chiffon. Her veil was decked with real orange blossoms, and she was also wearing as gifts of the bridegroom, a pearl and diamond necklace and diamond bracelets, and carrying a lovely shower bouquet of cream-coloured roses. Her four bridesmaids were Miss Agnes Nelson and Miss Florence Nelson, sisters, Miss Clarke, cousin of the bride, and Miss Breeze. Their dresses were all of green muslin, with transparent chiffon yokes and sleeves. They wore French hats, with drawn chiffon, green plumes, and osprey to match, and also gold chain bracelets, and carried green baskets of pink carnations, the gifts of the bridegroom. Mrs Nelson, mother of the bride, was among those who were present, and carried a bouquet of white roses and lilies. The best man was Mr R. Stratton, in the stead of Mr Percy Stevenson, of Birmingham, who was prevented at the last moment from attending owing to a sudden illness. The bride was given away by Mr Thomas Nelson, her brother, and the officiating clergyman was the Rev. A. T. Faber (curate). Mr Bonfield presided at the organ, and played the Wedding March during the fully choral service. Almost directly the ceremony was over, and they had responded to abundant congratulations, the wedding couple were driven to the Bedford L. & N.W. Station and by the 2.48 train started on their way to Scarborough, where the honeymoon is to be spent. From Scarborough they will proceed to Dover, and it is there that their future home will be established. Before they left Kempston, photographs of the groups had been taken by Messrs Bedwell & Brown, and there were nearly 60 guests at the reception held at the bride's home during the afternoon, a large marquee having been erected in the garden.

Among these guests were Miss Ford (Bickerton), Miss Baker, Mr James, Mr Jilks, Mr G. Trevis (Wood Green, London), Miss Payne, Mr and Mrs Harris, Mr and Mrs Payne, Miss E. Buck, Miss H. Robinson, Miss K. Robinson, Miss Wright, Mr A. Armsden, Mr F. Powell (Shaftesbury Theatre, London), Mr Fred. Southern, Miss Nitson, Mr Henry Kennersley, Mrs Kennersley, Miss Kennersley, Mr Edward Farden (uncle), Miss Toombs, Miss E. Toombs, Mrs R. Robinson, Miss R. M. Robinson, Mr and Mrs Lewin, Mr J. Robinson, Mrs J. Robinson, Mrs Stratton, and Miss Kitty Stratton.

Mr Charles Mann, of Silver-street, Bedford, was the caterer for the wedding breakfast.

The presents were the following:—

Bridegroom to bride, half hoop diamond bracelet, opal and diamond bracelet, gold necklet with diamond pendant, and dressing bag. Bride to bridegroom, silver-mounted hunting crop. Bridesmaids to bridegroom, silver-mounted driving whip. Father (Mr Nelson) to bride, brass swinging 5 o'clock tea kettle. Mother (Mrs Nelson), half dozen silver dessert spoons, etc., etc. Sister (Miss Nelson), 5 o'clock tea service. Sister (Miss Flo Nelson), olive-wood 5 o'clock tea tray and hand-worked cushion. Miss Clarke, cheese dish, d'oyleys, and pin cushion. Miss Maud Breeze (of Notts.), liqueur set. Miss Breeze (of Notts.), hand-painted, opal. Mrs Marion Breeze (of Nottingham), real Nottingham lace. Mr H. Farden, elaborate silk quilt and album. Mr H. Kennersley (uncle), brass bicycle bracket. Mrs H. Kennersley (aunt), standing work bag. Miss Kennersley (cousin), hair brushes. Miss Jessie Kennersley (cousin), set of vases. Miss Maud Kennersley (cousin), puss-in-boots and chicken salt cellar. Master Eddie Kennersley (cousin), pair of mounted plaques. Mr and Mrs Payne, set of carvers. Mr and Mrs Harris, double silver egg and toast rack. Mr S. Bell, silver teapot. Miss L. Wright, silver jam dish. Miss K. Robinson, silver cruet. Miss A. Robinson, butter dish, silver knife and jam spoon. Mrs Toombs and daughters, handsome silver jam dish. Mr Bert Armsden, hall barometer. Mrs R. Robinson and daughters, flower vase, salt cellars, horn-handled butter knife, and jam spoon. Mr Warden, mounted view. Mr and Mrs Edwards, bicycle basket. Miss E. Buck, glass water jug. Miss Symon, long silver button hook. Miss Folkes, pair of fans. Miss C. Folkes, ornaments. Miss M. Rogers, silver cruet. Mr and Mrs J. Robinson, silver cruet. Miss F. Baker and Mr G. James, silver-mounted double spirit flask. Mr G. Howe, Indian pin cushion. Miss F. Elsworth, pink facination. Mrs J. Braybrook, real Bedfordshire lace and handkerchief. Mr Reg. Stratton, clock. Mrs Bannister, hand bag. Miss Jessie Tilley, silver butter knife. Mrs Bonner, silver butter knife. Mrs Edwards (Northampton), sardine fork. Mr and Mrs Covington, silver-mounted walking-sticks. Mr Walter Green (London), pair of silver swans. Mr and Mrs Trevis (London), china timepiece. Friend, Staffordshire teapot and stand.

The report of the glittering wedding from the Bedfordshire Mercury, giving a list of the lavish gifts from the guests. The report fails to mention that Helen's father was absent but records that her brother gave her away. This leaves us to wonder if Isaac disapproved of the match.

If Isaac was hesitant about granting his daughter's hand in marriage to Edward Randell, he was very quickly proved right. The 'Dover Millionaire', as Edward was later described in a press cutting in the Kent papers, had a dubious history.

In the wedding report he had given the address of his father as Mark Lane in London. This is a prestigious address, a street in the city near the Tower of London, which at the time was the home of the London Corn Exchange, a very important establishment that set the price for wheat and other grains for most of the country.

At first the authors doubted that the name and address of Edward Randell senior on the marriage certificate could be true. The address seemed far too grand for a father who did not turn up to his son's wedding, but it turned out to be correct – Edward Randell had once been a well-to-do gentleman with a family business in Mark Lane.

The story of the bridegroom's early life is sad, and may explain Isaac Nelson's reluctance to welcome him as a son-in-law.

Edward Randell Smith was born on 29 January 1878, and at his baptism was registered with the father's name, given simply as Edward, and his surname as Smith, after his mother, Emily Jane Smith, who was thirty-two years younger than the boy's father and appears to have been his mistress.

Edward's parents did in fact marry three years later, on 26 May 1881, in St John's Church, Brixton, when the groom was 63 and the bride 31. The marriage was possible because Edward, who gave his profession as a malt factor, was a widower. He had outlived his first wife, although she had been considerably younger than him. Since she died in 1871, it is puzzling why he felt unable to marry Emily Jane before the birth of their son in 1878.

His new bride was a spinster, with her father being described as a soap manufacturer on the wedding certificate. However, Emily's family had fallen on hard times when she was a young child and she had been admitted to the workhouse at the age of 8, her father having died young and leaving her mother, three brothers and four sisters destitute.

The electoral register of 1881, the year of Edward Randell senior's second marriage, shows that he and Emily were living at The Elms, Acre Lane, Brixton, then a leafy outer suburb of London and still in the county of Surrey. The couple then moved to Knatchwell Road, Camberwell, but after nine years of marriage tragedy struck the young Edward when his father died at the age of 72. Edward Randell senior left an estate of £12,699, 11 shillings and 1 penny to his 40-year-old widow, equivalent to just over £1 million in today's money.

This large sum reflected his status as a man of property and the long lineage of the Randell family, who had been businessmen in the City of London for generations. He also left his gold watch and chain, furniture, linen, plate and plated articles, jewellery, pictures, books and other household and personal effects, liquor and consumable household stores, plus an immediate legacy of £100 cash to be paid on his death to his 'dear wife Emily'.

To John Charles Randell, his nephew, was bequeathed 'the old cabinet saved from the Great Fire of London 1666 and now in his charge and the oval oil painting of my grandfather James Randell now at 25 Mark Lane, aforesaid and I desire that the old cabinet and the oil painting always be kept in the Randell family'.

Along with another £370 of legacies, his widow was to receive the income from his investments to live on. When she died 'all the money, stocks and dividends to be paid to Edward Randell when he attains his 21st birthday on 29th January, 1899'. It appears that by this stage Edward junior is simply being called Edward Randell – the surname 'Smith' on his birth certificate having been dropped by the family; erasing the inconvenient fact that he was born before his parents were married.

Emily Jane and her teenage son continued to live in Camberwell and it appears that her nephew, William Lack, and one of her half-sisters, Matilda Ward, came to live with them.

But only three years after her husband's death, on 2 February 1894, Emily Jane died at the age of 43. It was three days after her son Edward's 16th birthday. Emily Jane, who had been receiving all the income from her husband's investments, left £1,558 15s 6d, a considerable sum for a girl from a workhouse. Apart from small bequests to her nephew and sister, the remainder of her estate was to pass to her son Edward, on his 21st birthday.

What happened to the orphaned Edward in the five years before he inherited the money is not known, but he appears to have made his way in the world and become a showman. By the time we rediscover him, the young Edward Randell had become a man about town – at least in Dover.

Two months before he married Helen in Kempston, and less than six months after his 21st birthday, an article appeared in *The Era*, a national weekly paper covering sport and theatre. On 17 June 1899 it described how 'Messrs Engleman and Randell had taken over the management from Mr and Mrs Joe Chevers' of the Chevers' Palace, Dover's music hall. Lavish gifts were exchanged between the old and new owners. Mrs Chevers was presented with a silver salver, silver purse, and diamond and ruby harp brooch from the new proprietors, 'also two handsome bouquets from admirers', while Mr Chevers received a 'silver cigar box, from the new proprietors; diamond pin, from patrons; meerschaum cigar holder, case of pipes, and cigar case, from staff and band'.

The Era reported, 'In a neat little speech Mrs Chevers introduced Messrs Engleman and Randell to the audience, and judging by the applause, these two gentleman already seemed very popular.' The band played 'Auld Lang Syne' and Mr and Mrs Chevers appeared in their own sketch entitled *Alphonso's Bride*. The paper also reported that in future, the music hall would be known as the Empire Palace of Varieties.

Two months later Edward Randell and Helen Nelson were married at Kempston. On the marriage certificate Edward's age was given as 24, although he was actually 21. His profession was given as 'proprietor' and his residence at the time of his marriage as the Empire, Dover. Helen's age was given as 20, although she was in fact just 19.

In view of future events it is worth noting that lavish gifts were reported at both the handing over of the ownership of the music hall and at the wedding. This, combined with the purchase of the music hall, suggests that Edward Randell was already spending a great deal of his inheritance.

2

BANKRUPTCY AND ABANDONMENT

After their honeymoon, Edward and Helen went to live at 3 East Cliff, Dover, a pleasant house overlooking the sea, and the future must have seemed rosy to the new Mrs Randell. Certainly, Edward was continuing to splash his money around and was the life and soul of any party. For example, in a report of the Dover Wednesday Cricket Club dinner of 3 November 1899, it was stated that once the meal was over 'the rest of the evening was devoted to toasts and song. The loyal toasts were enthusiastically honoured, Mr E. Randell, our Dover 'millionaire', standing champagne round for the purpose, and to spare. After this Mr Randell's own health was honoured, and musically. In replying, Mr Randell made a very humorous speech, concluding with the hope of long life for the Dover Wednesdays.'

But all was not as it seemed. It appears that while Edward Randell described himself as proprietor of the Empire Palace of Varieties, he had, along with his partner Jacob Engleman, only taken up a seven-year lease from Mr Chevers, from 12 June 1899, paying a rent of £150 per year. Engleman, who came from Birmingham, knew the business because he had previously been under-manager of the same music hall. He had then left and had successfully run the Lion Hotel in Dover, before returning to take a stake in the Empire.

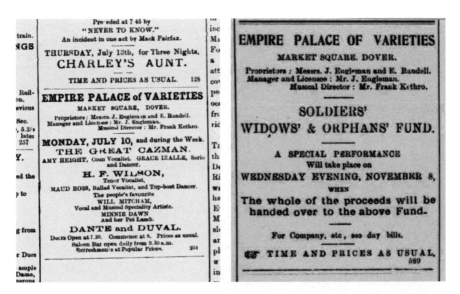

Two playbills published in the *Dover Express* advertising shows at the Empire Palace of Varieties, which show Edward Randell as joint proprietor. The first, from 7 July 1899, shows a classic music hall programme with The Great Cazman, and featuring Minnie Dawn and her pet lamb. The second, from November, is a benevolent fund event held in aid of the dependents of soldiers who had died in the Boer War, which had only begun the previous month. Soldiers waiting to embark for South Africa made up much of the music hall's audience.

How Edward Randell came to be in Dover remains a mystery, but perhaps it is more than a coincidence that both the best man, Percy Stevenson, who failed to turn up at Edward's wedding, and Mr Engleman came from Birmingham. Perhaps Edward had spent some time in Birmingham and met Engleman there, although it may be that he just used the name as a convenience since the authors' best efforts have failed to find anyone called Percy Stevenson in that part of the country.

In any case, the two partners had taken over and were running a very modern establishment in the Empire Palace of Varieties, also called the Empire Music Hall. According to the *Dover Express* at the time, the Empire claimed to have the 'best London artists' and 'electric light throughout', a rare thing in 1899. Seats cost between 6*d* (2.5 pence) and 10*s* (50p).

The pair purchased the fixtures and fittings for £1,000 – Engleman providing £400 and Randell £600.

Few pictures exist of the Empire
Palace of Varieties. The theatre
is on the left in this picture of
Market Square in Dover (*below*),
taken in about 1900. The grainy
picture shows how it looked
during the brief time Edward was
joint owner (*above*).

Whether Helen had any inkling of the problems ahead is not known, but less than five months after the couple set up home in Dover, Edward Randell disappeared. He was last seen in Dover on 23 January 1900, a week before his 22nd birthday.

It seems that by this time he was deep in debt, having run through the entire family fortune in less than twelve months. On 9 February, under the headline 'Millionaire Summoned', it was reported in the *Dover Express* that Edward Randell had been summonsed for non-payment of rates. The paper said: 'Defendant has been described as the Dover Millionaire and some time ago came into a large fortune. The clerk informed the Bench that Mr Randell had sailed for South Africa. The usual order was made.' In other words, the bailiffs would call at the defendant's home with an order to seize goods to the value of the rates owed.

Two weeks later, a notice of bankruptcy appeared in the *Dover Express*. The Official Receiver's notice said: 'Re. Edward Randell, lately carrying on business at the Empire Music Hall, Market Square, Dover, and residing at 3, East Cliff, Dover, Music Hall Proprietor. Receiving order made 20 February, 1900.' Events then moved quickly. On 6 March, in his absence, Edward Randell was adjudged bankrupt.

It is not known exactly how Helen parted from her husband, but she returned to the family home in Kempston – the King William IV public house. Nor is it known what possessions she managed to save from the marriage. She may have been able to keep the jewels she had been given 'as a gift from the groom' at her wedding, but if Edward had not paid for them yet then the Official Receiver would have claimed them.

At the time of her abandonment by her new husband, Helen was two months pregnant. Whether Edward knew he was to be a father is unknown.

In those straitlaced Victorian times, it must have been a difficult period for a young woman so publicly married at a glittering ceremony to return home just months later, pregnant and on her own. Her neighbours, and regulars at the pub, must have wondered what had happened. Did they know that the dashing young man had absconded and was being pursued by his creditors? While his bankruptcy had been reported in the Dover papers, there is no trace of it being publicly announced in Bedford.

REGISTRATION DISTRICT					BEDFORD				
1900 BIRTH in the Sub-district of Bedford and Kempston					in the County of Bedford				
Columns:-	1	2	3	4	5	6	7	8	9	10
No.	When and where born	Name, if any	Sex	Name and surname of father	Name, surname and maiden surname of mother	Occupation of father	Signature, description and residence of informant	When registered	Signature of registrar	Name entered after registration
3/6	Sixteenth August 1900 High Street Kempston U.D	Irene Nelson	Girl	Edward Randell	Helen Randell formerly Nelson	Music Hall Proprietor	H Randell mother High Street Kempston	Third October 1900	Wm Payne Registrar	

The birth certificate of Irene Nelson, Edward and Helen's daughter, who was born in the King William IV seven months after her father disappeared. Helen lists the father's occupation as 'music hall proprietor' despite knowing that he has been declared bankrupt.

Helen's baby, Irene, was born on 16 August 1900 at Kempston. The father is given as Edward Randell, music hall proprietor, and the mother's address as High Street, Kempston.

The statements on the birth certificate are not strictly true because by that time Edward had been gone for more than six months, had been declared bankrupt, and his share in the music hall bought out by his partner from the Official Receiver for £400, the money being used to pay off some of his other creditors.

What happened to Edward remains a mystery. At the time foreign travel did not require passports and it would have been quite easy for Edward to simply pack a bag, catch the ferry from Dover to the continent, and disappear.

Alternatively, his disappearance was at the height of the Boer War, when many ships were going to South Africa. The opportunities for a young Englishman to change his name back to Smith and start a new life without too many awkward questions being asked must have been excellent.

3

HELEN MARRIES AGAIN

Whatever the locals may have been told, or knew, Helen and her new baby remained in Kempston at the King William IV, the young mother no doubt helping out in what was a large and busy public house. The 1901 census shows the child, Irene N. Randell, aged 7 months, living at 36 High Street (the address of the King William IV) with her mother Ellen Randell, aged 22 and described as married. Also living in the pub was Ellen's unmarried sister Florence, aged 24, her father Isaac, a licensed victualler, and his wife Kate Nelson. Isaac was aged 63 and Kate was 53.

The next news we have of the family is on 22 May 1903, when Kate Nelson dies aged 55. The *Bedfordshire Times* reported: 'We regret to announce the death of Mrs Nelson, wife of the esteemed host of the King William Inn, who died on Friday morning after a painful illness. Much sympathy has been expressed with Mr Nelson and his family in their bereavement.'

Despite the loss of his wife, Isaac and his two daughters continued to run the pub.

Tragedy struck again two years later when Isaac had a fall. The local paper reported that on 2 August 1905 an inquest was held into the death of Isaac Nelson, landlord of the King William IV, Kempston. Ellen Randell was the chief witness, describing how her father, aged 66, 'who had been ailing a long time' but was able to get about, had a fall outside

A LICENSED VICTUALLER'S BANKRUPTCY

RE EDWARD SWINDFORD FRY, LICENSED VICTUALLER, SANDWICH, FORMERLY OF DOVER.

The Official Receiver said that the deficiency was returned at £435, but it would not be so much as that, as he had disposed of licensed premises for the debtor. Debtor stated that he commenced business in 1893, taking the Ancient Druids at Stembrook, Dover. He then had a capital of £135, borrowed from his mother, which was still outstanding. That was always a good house, and for seven years he carried on the business successfully. During a portion of that time he had certain contracting rights in connection with the Athletic Grounds, but he disposed of them in the latter part of 1899 for £250, which sum was paid by a cheque of Edward Randell, the "Dover millionaire," who became bankrupt in that court and went away, and had never been seen since.

The Official Receiver said it was believed he went to South Africa.

Continuing, debtor said he used to pay £20 a year for the right of catering and supplying refreshments, but he never made anything out of it. On leaving the Ancient Druids he took Ye Olde New Inn, Sandwich, the valuation of which was £290, £240 of which was provided by the cheque Randell gave him. The balance of the £290 was provided out of the money he received in respect of the valuation of the Ancient Druids. This left the sum of £150 balance in his hands with which he paid his Dover creditors. On the 14th of February last he gave a bill of sale over his effects for £220, and in this sum was included the amount of the dishonoured cheque given him by Randell. The bill of sale had been abandoned. He was insolvent 18 months ago when he left the Ancient Druids.

A cutting from the *Dover Express* of 7 June 1901, recording the bankruptcy of the former landlord of the Ancient Druids public house, Dover, in which he recounts selling a catering business to the 'Dover Millionaire' Edward Randell, who disappeared following his bankruptcy. The Official Receiver says Randell is believed to have gone to South Africa.

the back door of the pub the previous Friday evening. Two men had gone to his assistance but the Isaac said he had hurt himself and the doctor was called.

The following day he was removed to hospital, where he was found to have a broken thigh. He was put in splints but Mr Nelson became delirious and violent, and heart failure followed.

A few days later Isaac was buried at the Kempston Cemetery 'amid many tokens of respect'. In addition to the relatives, a number of friends were present. Mr Nelson had been a well-known publican in the town for twelve years.

Isaac Nelson's death created a crisis for the remaining members of the family. They would have to leave the pub quickly because the owners needed to appoint a new resident licensee to carry on the business. In the

Helen's second marriage certificate, in which she describes herself as a widow, although there is no evidence that her first husband had died. Her sister, who is a witness, must have colluded in this bigamous marriage.

records Jack Evans took over the license in that year, although the precise date is not known.

Events moved swiftly. There was a sale of Isaac Nelson's effects on 21 September 1905. The contents of the pub included 'antique and modern household furniture, Dog Cart, 100 head of poultry etc.' by direction of the representatives of the late Isaac Nelson.

Five days later, on 26 September, Helen married again. This marriage certainly came at a convenient moment for the young mother, being on the back of losing both her father and her home.

The groom was a 26-year-old Bertie Benjamin MacVicar Armstrong, the son of a Lincolnshire doctor. His occupation was given as a horse breaker, a respectable profession, and his address was Adelaide Square in Bedford.

Helen gave her address as 36 High Street, Kempston, so at the time of her marriage she was still living in the pub. At the time of her daughter's birth in 1900, and in the census of 1901, she had described herself as married but, remarkably, was described on the wedding certificate four years later as a widow, although there is no record of Edward Randell's death. As far as the authorities in Dover were concerned, Edward was reported to have become bankrupt and absconded, probably to South Africa, so this marriage could be described as bigamous.

One of the two witnesses to the marriage was Helen's older sister Florence, who had also been a long-term resident at the pub. Perhaps with her mother dead, and her ex-policeman father no longer there to remind her of her past mistakes, Helen's two sisters and brother Thomas conspired to conceal the fact that Edward Randell was probably still alive. In those days each county kept its own records of marriages and deaths, so there was no way of cross-checking whether entries on marriage certificates were accurate. Although it was a criminal offence – with a potential prison sentence – to give incorrect information, if her sisters and brother remained silent, who was to know?

Back in Dover, the effects of Edward's bankruptcy were still being felt. For some years after his disappearance, a series of bankruptcy hearings were heard. Edward (again described as the Dover Millionaire) had paid £250 by cheque for a catering contract with Dover Athletic Grounds but had subsequently 'become bankrupt and went away, and had never been seen since'. At this hearing in June 1901, the Official Receiver said it was believed that Randell had gone to South Africa, and there had been no news of him since his disappearance.

Edward's partner, Jacob Engleman, had also been forced into bankruptcy in November 1901, in part due to an attempt to rescue the music hall business from the financial disaster that Edward Randell left behind.

Engleman had unsecured liabilities of £1,196 and assets of only £459, leaving a deficiency of £737. He put the failure of the business of the Empire Palace of Varieties down to 'Bad Trade in consequence of the fine weather and the absence of troops from Dover'. This observation ties in with many of the troops being sent to South Africa to reinforce the army. Engleman described how his problems began when he had entered into partnership with Edward Randell in the proprietorship of the Empire Palace of Varieties.

The Official Receiver, in the course of his observations on the bankruptcy, said that part of Engleman's problem was that his partner Edward Randell had absconded and been declared bankrupt in his absence. Engleman had acquired Randell's share of the business for £400, a sum that he had borrowed, and this money was still outstanding.

It was not until July 1904 that this series of bankruptcy hearings were wound up, when the Official Receiver declared a third and final dividend to Edward Randell's creditors on an outstanding debt of more than £1,000.

Four years after his disappearance, there were still no further clues given by the Official Receiver to Edward's whereabouts, and he was still assumed to have absconded to South Africa to escape his creditors. The Boer War was over by then but he had not returned, or at least no one in Dover had seen him.

How many of these events Helen was able to follow from Kempston is not known, but it seems likely that she would have been informed. After all, the Official Receiver would have had to decide what personal effects she could keep, and which of the couple's possessions should be sold to help pay off Edward's debts. It is also possible that he had some remaining assets, which she would have been entitled to.

By the time Helen remarried, she would have had plenty of time to have formed her views on her first husband's behaviour. It is possible, having known him for such a short time, that she never really knew who he was, and after his disappearance, whether he was alive or dead. Either way, he seems to have vanished, completely abandoning his new bride and baby daughter.

Regardless, Helen put her first marriage behind her and began a new life. Her parents were dead, but she and her daughter were safely under the protection of a new husband and ready to start all over again.

4

THE TODDINGTON LANDLADY

Up to this point Helen may be described as headstrong, but she also appears to have had a lot of bad luck. In the Victorian era, for a woman to be abandoned by a new husband was socially disgraceful. But for a pregnant bride to be abandoned by a new husband who left behind a string of debts, with no assets and no home, it was catastrophic.

That Helen survived at all is a tribute to her strength of character. The motives for her second marriage, so rapidly after losing her father and her home in the pub, are perhaps for the readers to decide.

What follows, however, is entirely down to Helen. The next twelve years would be tumultuous by anyone's standards. Her love letters reveal that Helen led a complicated life. This was made a lot worse by the fact that the three new men in her life all ended up serving as officers on the front line in the First World War.

To attract such men, all of whom seem to have courageously served their country, there must have been something special about Helen. Sadly, we do not have a photograph of her in her youth, but we do know from her letters that she was very conscious of the fact that she had to look young and pretty. She was worried that as she got older, the man she really loved would not want her anymore.

***

We take up her story again in July 1907 when the newly married Mr and Mrs Armstrong took over the licence of the Sow and Pigs, a large public house and hotel in Toddington, Bedfordshire. As far as we know, Bertie Armstrong, the horse breaker, had no experience of running hostelries and must have been relying on his new wife to teach him.

At the time he took over the licence, Bertie gave his address as Church Square, Toddington, which is the same address as the pub, so he was already living there.

Although the pub was only about 12 miles from Kempston, this tenancy marks a complete break from Helen's old life. From her letters it is clear that she is in charge of this new establishment, and has her own staff. The couple were renting the pub from the Wells and Winch brewery at £33 a year. Although one of a number of inns in Toddington, it was one of the largest. Downstairs it had a bar and tap room, a commercial room,

The Sow and Pigs advertising good stabling. This picture was taken in 1905, the year Helen and Bertie got married, and two years before they took over the hotel. On the left is the Bell Inn, one of the ten other pubs in the village at about this time. The large tree on the right is in the churchyard.

reception room, kitchen, larder and pantry. Upstairs was a billiard room, six bedrooms (including four to let), a bathroom and WC. Outside was two lots of brick-and-tile stables for a number of horses, a coach house, timber-and-thatch barn and loft, brick-and-tile warehouse, saddle room and a garden with a plum tree.

The hotel and its landlord and landlady are referred to in a book called *Toddington Memories* by local man Robert Victor Holman Seymour. In a chapter in which he details the importance of horses in the village before the First World War, he describes how Toddington had a Company of Yeomanry, which practised at Woburn Park:

> The same riders with the same horses were, of course, to be seen at the hunt, although the sport was declining in the district probably because there were fewer aristocratic land owners left who could afford the expense that a hunt entailed. It was also usual to find a good hostelry somewhere in the neighbourhood, where groups could join, or collect their horses, or have a refresher before or after the immediate business of the hunt. Such a hostelry was the Sow and Pigs in Toddington kept by a man familiarly known as Bertie Armstrong, and his wife. It had stables at the back that were reached by a cobbled entrance, across the road was the church, and one realised that here was the heart and soul of Toddington, refreshment for mind and body. How the iron shod hoofs of the horses rang on those cobbles interspersed with the farmers' cries of 'Whoa, Stand still then' as they tried to hold their horse with one hand, and balance their pint of ale in the other without spilling it.

The Sow and Pigs was a prestigious establishment that attracted distinguished visitors. A year after Bertie and Helen took over, the *Luton Times* of August 1908 reported the overnight visit to the hotel of Dorando Pietri, the Olympic marathon runner, and his brother, Ulpiano, who was also his trainer. The Italian had just won the marathon at the London Olympics and was a celebrity, although he was later disqualified. The brothers 'had motored over from Luton, putting up at the Sow and Pigs. The hostess Mrs Armstrong produced her visitors' book, which the visitors signed, afterwards expressing themselves delighted with the natural beauties of the place.'

The Parish Church opposite the hotel has a number of animals and other decorations in stone. This restored carving of a sow and pigs replaces an earlier version and is exactly opposite the hotel – clearly the origin of the name of the establishment.

THE GREEN TODDINGTON.

The village green, Toddington, taken in 1909, when Helen and Bertie were running the hotel. On the left of the green is what appears to be a traditional maypole. The children are playing where the 1914–18 war memorial now stands.

High Street, Toddington, as it looked in about 1910 when Helen was already landlady of the Sow and Pigs. The view is towards Dunstable. On the left is a forge with a knife-grinding machine. The chimney in the background belongs to the local brewery.

Bertie Armstrong, as well as being the licensee, continued with his horse-breaking business and was joined enthusiastically by his new wife, who clearly attracted attention. In 1909 the following report appeared in the *Luton Times and Advertiser*: 'Local prize winners in the Bedfordshire Agricultural Show at Ampthill included Mr B McVicar Armstrong's chestnut gelding "Ginger Hot" which won third prize. The pony was driven by Mrs Armstrong, who received quite an ovation from the crowd, she being the only lady at the show who drove in any competition.'

But it also appears that Helen was left to carry out most of the administration and organisation at the hotel, where quite a number of the traditional dinners and meetings of Toddington took place. In the *Luton Times* there is mention of the Court Leet (the ancient court of Toddington Manor) held in May 1911, where, in the 'large room of The Sow and Pigs Hotel the quaint old customs were duly observed. Dinner was well served by Mrs Armstrong.'

In the census of that year Bertie, aged 29, is described as the 'hotel proprietor', and his wife, Helen, aged 30, as assisting in the business. Irene Nelson Randell, 'stepdaughter', is 10, widow Louisa Bonner, aged 37, is

Toddington High Street looking towards the church and the village green, behind which is the Sow and Pigs and the road to Bedford, which passes between the two. The picture was taken in about 1903 and shows the unmade road.

described as housekeeper of the hotel, and Agnes Wright, aged 28, single as a general servant, domestic.

It soon becomes obvious that after five years the marriage was not going well. Helen and her new husband did not have any children and in May 1913 Bertie went to Canada with some of his horses, and did not return.

One of the few documents that Helen held on to for the rest of her life was the 'Publican's Licence and Tobacco Licence' for the house in Toddington, known 'by the sign of the Sow and Pigs.' The licence, which allowed for the selling of beer, spirits, tobacco and snuff, was originally granted to Bertie MacVicar Armstrong but a note signed by J.R. Jackson, from Customs & Excise, reads, 'We hereby transfer this licence to Helen Armstrong this 26th day of September 1913.' So Helen was left in sole charge of running the Sow and Pigs, quite a responsibility, but she also found time for recreation.

From the love letters it is clear that soon after her husband went to Canada, she acquired a boyfriend called Tommy. What Tommy did for a living before the war, or how serious this relationship was is not known, but he continued to contact her and when Helen acquired a new lover she had to ask Tommy to stay away from Toddington. Fortunately for her, Tommy was posted a long way away – as a staff officer in the Yeomanry Brigade, Western Frontier Force, in Alexandria, Egypt.

In 1913, a year before war broke out, Helen decided to ditch Tommy when she met another man – the love of her life, James Norbury Franklin-Smith. According to her love letters, they met during a chance encounter at the Leighton Buzzard Horse Show, but there was an instant attraction, and a kiss. It seems to have been love at first sight on both sides.

The event on 14 August 1913 was a large competitive horse-riding show organised by the banker, Mr Evelyn de Rothschild, whose family still live in the village of Ascott near Wing, 2 miles from Leighton. He funded the local staghounds, at which the Prince of Wales was a frequent rider and guest of the Rothschilds. The horse show was held at Bridge Meadows, the area of water meadows sandwiched between the canal and River Ouzel, and Linslade and Leighton. It featured competitors from all over the country.

Helen and Franklin-Smith's first meeting soon blossomed into a full-blown affair. Their meeting and subsequent courtship is frequently mentioned in the letters, to remind each other of how happy they were before the war separated them.

Frank, as Helen called him, when she was not using pet names, appears to have been part of a high-class firm of auctioneers, Norbury Smith and Co., who ran sales at the Sugar Loaf Hotel in Dunstable and had an office in the town. He had lodgings in Dunstable, but according to the love letters, soon moved to a room in the Sow and Pigs, with frequent visits to the landlady's bedroom.

Like Helen, Frank was prone to changing his name and personal details on documents. He was plain Franklin Smith on his baptism register and on his own entry on the 1911 census but seems to have added Norbury, one of his grandmother's maiden names, to make the auctioneers business sound posh. Later he amended his name again and became James Franklin-Smith.

5

War Changes Everything

There is no record of Bertie returning to Britain during 1913. And while we do not know what the state of Helen and Bertie's relationship was when he left for Canada, we do know that Helen continued to run the hotel, and that she and Frank were left alone to continue their affair. This arrangement appears to have continued for a year until the outbreak of the First World War, when Bertie arrived back in Britain with the patriotic purpose of joining up to fight for his country.

How Helen organised her life when Bertie returned is not clear, but she repeatedly claimed to Frank in her love letters that she had never been a 'wife' to her husband after his return and that she always remained loyal to her lover.

Although Frank might also have enlisted or returned to his lodgings in Dunstable when Bertie came back from Canada, it is clear that he continued to maintain a room at the Sow and Pigs because some of the clothes he did not need in the army were stored there during the war, along with other possessions. Bertie could not have been aware of the couple's affair.

The declaration of war changed everyone's lives, and Toddington, like so many other places, was gripped with war fever. Men, many of whom were employed in the local cement works, rushed to enlist, presenting themselves to the local GP, Dr Waugh, for medical examination. They were joined by volunteers from Tebworth and Wingfield. About fifty young men from a population of just under 2,000 joined up immediately. They were marched through the town (Toddington was described as a town in those days) on the way to Harlington station singing the First World War song 'It's a Long Way to Tipperary'. Helen must have watched from the window of the Sow and Pigs or perhaps stood outside and waved them goodbye, wondering what would happen to them. At the time, the general view was that the war would be over by Christmas. No one knew that the conflict would continue for four long years.

Bertie returned home in September 1914, a month after war broke out, and joined up three weeks later. Having previously served in South Africa, being a good horseman, and 'with some experience of military life', he was accepted in the King Edward's Horse and sent to France in April 1915.

It must have been a severe shock to these soldiers. Like so many cavalry regiments their role changed dramatically because of the nature of trench warfare, and these men had to fight on foot. Among the battles they were involved in were Loos and Ypres, before being sent to Italy and then returning to France to defend the La Basse Canal near Hinges, where the regiment had 60 per cent casualties.

Bertie returned to the Sow and Pigs several times whilst on leave and also en route to Ireland, where the regiment had a recruiting and training base. The regiment also helped restore order in the Irish Troubles in 1916. During those visits to the hotel Helen's refusal to accept Bertie back into her bedroom angered him. Relations between husband and wife were clearly strained and Helen could not wait for him to go away again. She also discovered during this period that her husband had love letters from women in Canada and Ireland.

In contrast to her frosty relationship with Bertie, the letters she writes to Frank at his various postings in France and later Salonika in Greece are remarkably intimate and full of desperate longing. So keen are they not to miss a single word from each other that Frank even asks what the words were that Helen had crossed out in a previous letter. Also, both begin to number their letters to make sure none are lost in the post.

Helen frequently addresses Frank as her husband and repeatedly says she wants to have his children. She is anxious to get married as soon as possible, although this prospect must have seemed a long way off. She also signs these letters 'Nell' rather than Helen.

Helen's monogram on the top of her early letters – NMA. This must stand for Nell MacVicar-Armstrong, her married name. She signs her love letters 'Nell', although on her wedding certificate her name is Helen.

The first of the 100 love letters is addressed to Frank in France, where he had been posted after training in England. Helen's passion for Frank is obvious in the way she starts and ends this first letter. She calls him her husband, and signs off as his wife, although she is married to someone else.

The letters are initially addressed to Captain Franklin Smith, Commanding Cyclist Company of the 22nd Division of the British Expeditionary Force in France. A short time later, Frank and the British Cyclist Company was posted to Salonika. (This is now Greece's second city and a major port known as Thessaloniki, although it can be spelled a number of ways.) In the First World War it was a dangerous place to be, mainly because of the prevalence of malaria and other diseases that claimed more lives than the fighting – although there was plenty of that too.

Frank caught one of these diseases and ended up in hospital in December 1915. Since he was living in a tent – and from his requests for socks and thick underwear – it is clear it was very cold and perhaps not surprising therefore that he succumbed to illness. A number of envelopes show that Helen's letters were redirected from company headquarters to local hospitals and he appears to have spent most of the month recovering. There is no evidence that he was wounded and Helen refers in her letters to his illness, although the exact nature of his infirmity is not known.

The pair appear to have written to each other several times a week and their letters must have crossed in the post. The army post office worked hard to ensure letters from home reached the men. One registered letter from Helen, postmarked as being dispatched in Toddington on 7 December, had three army postmarks on the back for 17, 20, and 21 December until they found him and managed to deliver it to the General Canadian Hospital in Salonika.

The job of the Cyclist Company was to carry messages between the different allied forces on the front who were fighting the Bulgarians and Turks. The 22nd Division was formed in September 1914 from volunteers, shortly after the outbreak of the war. Twelve months later, after training, the division, including Frank's company, was sent to France and then in October 1915 to Greece.

From the letters, it is clear that Frank had been in the army some time before he was posted to France, and with Bertie already in France it was possible for the lovers to meet when Frank was on leave.

There is a repeated reference by Helen to one of these trysts when she travelled to London to meet Frank, but they did not spend much time together. The reasons for this are not given, but Helen constantly chides him about his behaviour on this occasion, which is rare. Apart from con-

ARE **YOU** FOND OF CYCLING?

IF SO

WHY NOT CYCLE FOR THE KING?

RECRUITS WANTED

By the S. Midland Divisional Cyclist Company

(Must be 19, and willing to serve abroad).

CYCLES PROVIDED. Uniform and Clothing issued on enlistment.

Application in person or by letter to Cyclists, The Barracks, Gloucester.

BAD TEETH NO BAR.

H. Osborne, Printer, St. Mary's Square, Gloucester.

Horses were very vulnerable on the battlefield so they were rapidly replaced by cyclists carrying messages from the front line to headquarters. Although Frank commanded a cyclist company, he apparently still had a horse in Salonika as he asked Helen for a new set of spurs because his had been stolen. This poster has a rather strange appeal to people with bad teeth.

> TODDINGTON,
> DUNSTABLE.
> September 7th 1915
>
> Frank my own darling
>
> I got a letter from you yesterday morning Monday was it not jolly nice kid? I was so glad it was the last letter from Aldershot the one you wrote at 2 a.m. Saturday morning you darling Frank you did send me some topping letters last week thank you so much but you do know how much your letters mean to me so you will understand just how I feel about them but to get a letter from you Monday morning knowing you were in France was more than I expected & I loved it, I was not out of bed when Mrs Bonner brought me the letter I read it & then just cuddled it up to me right inside my Nighty

stantly urging that he should write more often, her letters are largely about her desperation to be with him again. She also worries about the fact he might get hurt or ill, and that she will not be there to nurse him.

The difficulties of sending parcels containing items Frank needed for his comfort at the front is detailed. For example, there is the refusal of the Post Office to take the parcels tied up with string and the insistence that they are stitched in linen, which delayed their dispatch.

5 badly we have both agreed that we should have we not? I shall want this baby because if afterwards anything happened to you I could always look at him & know he was yours. Our baby Frank do you understand? do you know how much I love you when I think & write like this.

I must finish now sweetheart mine, please write to me & tell me you love me.

My darling, Frank!

Your very own wife Nell

Two extracts from Helen's many intimate letters to Frank. The first, early in their correspondence, tells him that she is 'cuddling it [the letter] up to me right inside my nighty' and the second, much later, that she wants his baby if 'anything happened to you'.

One of the complications of them keeping track of each other is that letters included in parcels containing tobacco, boots and such items as spurs, took longer to reach their destination than letters posted on their own. Looking back from this distance, it seems remarkable that both the soldier at the front and the landlady of a hotel were able to write to each other two or three times a week and expect their letters and parcels to be delivered reliably by a postal service operating across war-torn Europe.

From the letters it is clear that there was great passion on both sides. Despite the difficult and dangerous conditions that Frank found himself in in Salonika, he was as eager to receive letters and write them as Helen was in Toddington.

Helen confesses herself miserable in Toddington and relates that business at the Sow and Pigs was poor. She says that some days there were

The Signals Section of the Royal Engineers outside Toddington Post Office. They were billeted in Toddington between February and May 1915, and must have provided a source of income for the local pubs.

almost no customers and she barely took 2*s* 6*d* all evening. At other times she had army guests to stay and was very busy, but, in general, trade was bad. This was partly because so many potential male customers were at the front but also because the government, fearful of excessive drinking among soldiers on leave, had restricted pub opening hours and actively discouraged alcohol consumption.

Among the army guests were officers from the Royal Engineers who came with all their equipment to Toddington. Most of the men were billeted with local households. In his book, *Toddington Memories*, Seymour says that two of them stayed in his home and it was 'good fun'. The soldiers were training in telecommunications and went out each day to practise laying cables across the countryside, a prelude to keeping headquarters in touch with the trenches on the Western Front.

The cables were wound on great drums mounted on heavy army wagons or carriages. After laying the cables and making sure the telephones worked, the soldiers wound them back up again. Much of the heavy work of pulling the wagons was done by teams of six horses and the engineers had to look after them, keeping them well fed, stabled and groomed. Surplus hay to feed them was requisitioned from the farmers by the army, whose requirements had priority.

Frank asks what life is like in Toddington but Helen does not give him much news, apart from the fact that the village policeman's move to Leighton Buzzard had been delayed, because the authorities were having difficulty finding a house big enough for him and his thirteen children.

To give some idea of local concerns, the *Luton News* reported in 1915: 'A parish meeting has been held at Toddington to discuss whether street lamps should continue to be lit in view of the threat posed by Zeppelins.' Dr Waugh, Chairman of the Parish Council, felt that while Toddington itself was not likely to be in danger of German bombs, as it was one of the highest points in the county, the lights could serve as a guide to other places. As the rates had already been set and the council was under contract to the gas company, a decision not to light the lamps would not lead to a reduction in the amount payable. After some discussion it was decided that the lamps would still be lit, but the tops would be darkened and they would be extinguished at 9 o'clock instead of 10 o'clock.

On 11 November 1915 Helen wrote:

How are you Frank dear, are you quite well and fairly happy? I hope you are. My darling you have no real idea as to what Toddington is like now, night after night we have no one in not even one single person and even out of doors no lights visible, is it not too ridiculous, the lights from the houses have had to be to a certain extent darkened but that makes not the slightest difference to me because I never go out after dark with the exception to the letter box and even that I cannot find without groping for it.

She does tell of one war-related excursion with her daughter, Irene, who she rather curiously calls 'Bob', which also shows to what lengths she went to keep her relationship with Frank a secret:

Such excitement just now, Frank dear, a balloon over Toddington which appeared to be coming down, so I said to Bob come along kid let us go, so off we started then we saw Ruffett tearing off on his old motor bike with side car so we shouted please give us a ride (do not forget that I had not explained to Rose we were going out). He pulled up and we packed in, right

away down the Tingrith lane we went, and then we ran over three huge
fields and got there just as they were rolling up the canvas, quite a number of
people had arrived from the village before we got there. Six naval men were
with the balloon, one or two of them quite nice looking boys, please do not
be jealous. Anyway, Bob and I thoroughly enjoyed our little pleasure trip,
particularly the ploughed field. I left this letter of yours half finished but had
the presence of mind to lock the C. Room door and take the key with me.
For today my darling I must finish. Goodbye my husband-to-be, I love you.
Always your very own Nell.

Some domestic issues are also discussed, including the dangerous illness of
Louisa Bonner, the housekeeper, who happened to be away from the Sow
and Pigs because her fiancé, Horace Frederick Fletcher, was on leave. This
was a lucky break for Helen because diphtheria is infectious. Mrs Bonner
was sent to the local fever hospital.

Sweetheart mine you will be sorry to hear that Mrs Bonner is suffering from
Diphtheria and was taken to the Fever Hospital on Saturday morning last.
I am pleased to say I had not seen anything of her for several days beforehand
as Horace Fletcher has been home and she never or very seldom comes
anywhere near me when he is here, I think she much dislikes for me to see
them together, he was at home when the Doctor pronounced it Diphtheria
so of course his leave is extended, I think they say for a fortnight.

The Diphtheria is really very bad in the village, fresh cases nearly every
day. I felt rather merry when I heard about Mrs Bonner and felt jolly pleased
I had not been in her company. I do not know what I should do kid if I got
badly down with anything like that, but as I tell Rose not under any circumstances shall I be taken to the Fever Hospital.

Throughout her letters Helen complains that she is short of money, yet
despite this she sends Bob, now aged 14, away to boarding school at Howard
College in Bedford. It is quite clear that before the war Bob had already
developed a friendship with Frank, as it is mentioned in the love letters that
the two of them also exchange letters and Frank sends her presents. Helen
encourages their friendship.

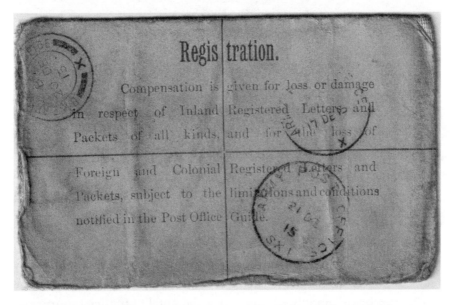

The front and back of a registered letter sent to Frank from Helen in Toddington, posted at 5.45 p.m. on 9 December 1915 at the cost of 2*d*. The back showed it arrived in Greece on 17 December but two more postmarks on 20 and 21 December show that the army had trouble tracking Frank down. He was probably still in hospital at this time.

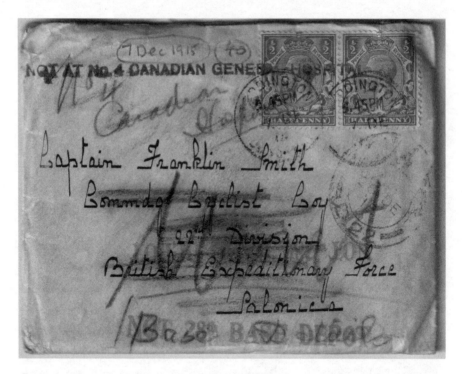

This envelope shows the tortuous journey Helen's letter must have taken to reach Frank. Certainly the army postal service went to great lengths to make sure the mail arrived. The letter was posted on 7 December 1915 but on the back there is another postmark showing that the army in Greece was still looking for Frank on 3 January 1916. It seems that by then he had been discharged from the Canadian hospital and rejoined his unit.

Money, or rather lack of it, and bills that have not been paid, are frequently discussed in the letters. Helen fears getting into debt because takings at the hotel do not cover her expenditure.

Helen is anxious to leave the Sow and Pigs, divorce her husband, marry Frank and have his babies, but realises this will not be possible until the war is over. Frank urges her to remain at the hotel until they can sort out their future.

Because of the lack of business and her inability to make ends meet, Helen decides, after much hesitation, to discharge her housekeeper Mrs Bonner, who had been at the pub for some years. She was described as resident housekeeper in the 1911 census and clearly from comments in the letters knew all about Helen's affair with Frank.

Mrs Bonner seems to have married Horace in the summer of 1915 but continued to live in at the pub, asking for nights off when her new husband came home on leave. Helen is not very complimentary about Mrs Bonner's appearance in her letters but was reluctant to lose her help in running the hotel, leaving her with only one live-in servant, Rose, for assistance.

To stave off her financial problems, Frank regularly sends Helen cheques from the front. This also enables her to keep Bob at school in Bedford.

While Bertie, who is in France and then in Ireland, seems to have opportunities to come home to the Sow and Pigs on leave or whilst in transit, it appears that Frank, much further away in Salonika, has no chance to do so. Helen frequently asks for news of when he is coming home, but there does not appear to be any prospect when the sequence of letters suddenly ends. The last one is dated 1 July 1916.

It seems certain that the two lovers continued to write to each other but only the 100 letters reproduced in this book appear to have survived.

What sparse information there is about the complicated lives of Frank, Bertie and Helen between this date and the end of the war can only be pieced together from official documents. In Frank's case, his unit was amalgamated into the British VXI Corps in January 1916 and became one of two British Divisions within the British Salonika Army. This became a very similar battleground to the Western Front, with close fighting over trenches and gun emplacements, with the added hazard of mosquitoes. Evidently promotion followed, because by the end of the war Frank had achieved the rank of Lieutenant Colonel.

A little more is known about Bertie, who received the Military Cross 'for conspicuous gallantry and devotion to duty'. The citation in the *London Gazette* for 22 June 1918 reads: 'When the horse lines of two troops were heavily shelled he at once went to the spot and encouraged and assisted his men in the difficult task of getting the horses away. By his energy, promptness and disregard of danger he succeeded in accomplishing this with very few casualties.'

The *Bedfordshire Times and Independent* for 19 July of that year reported that Bertie had been promoted to Acting Captain of his company and had on several occasions been highly commended by his superiors before being awarded the Military Cross for distinguished service in the field. The paper then quotes the citation before saying that 200 men had gone to the front

Peace Day celebrations in 1918. The children are being treated to tea on Toddington village green. Helen must have been celebrating too, because it meant she could now divorce Bertie and marry Frank.

from Toddington and forty had made 'the supreme sacrifice'. 'Toddington feels honoured by its brave men who are thus gallantly defending their homes and fatherland.'

When the war ended months later, the two men in Helen's life came home. Helen was quick off the mark as soon as peace was restored: ten days after Armistice, on 21 November 1918, she petitioned the High Court for the end of her marriage to Bertie. She stated that, 'your petitioner then Helen Randell, widow, was on the 26th day of 1905 married to Benjamin Bertie MacVicar Armstrong at Bedford Register Office. She had lived with him at the Sow and Pigs Toddington but there were no children of the marriage.'

The Sow and Pigs in the early 1920s, shortly after Helen had married Frank and moved away from Bedfordshire to spend the next thirty-four years with the love of her life.

In a statement she then accused her husband of abusing her in front of the servants, throwing a lighted oil lamp at her and 'striking her and violently assaulting her so that the petitioner has suffered great pain both mentally and physically'.

She also accused him of 'deserting her without cause for two years and upwards'. During the years 1913 and 1914 her husband 'lived and cohabited in Canada with a woman who was not your petitioner and habitually committed adultery with her there'.

She also accused, 'on 26th day of October 1918 he had committed adultery with a woman called Sharp at a flat in Carlton Mansions, 178 Shaftsbury Avenue in London.'

At the end of the petition she signed a statement, which affirmed all her allegations were true and added: 'There is no collusion or connivance between me and my husband the said Benjamin Bertie MacVicar Armstrong in any way whatsoever.' Bertie does not seem to have made any attempt to refute any of these allegations and the petition resulted in an uncontested divorce.

The Sow and Pigs was closed in 2011. This blue plaque placed on the wall reminds people of the building's history.

The Sow and Pigs in 2018, after conversion to a dentist's surgery.

The account of the court proceedings carried in the *Bedfordshire Times and Independent* of 9 May 1919 says Mrs Helen Armstrong petitioned for a decree to dissolve her marriage with Captain Benjamin Bertram Armstrong because of his alleged desertion, cruelty and misconduct.

Mr Acton Pile, appearing on behalf of Mrs Armstrong, was therefore unchallenged when he said:

The marriage turned out unhappy from the start, and in May 1913 her husband went to Canada with some horses. When he came back in September

1914, she noticed a considerable change in him, but he told her nothing to account for it.

Three weeks later he joined the Army, went to France in May 1915. He did not say good-bye to her and between November 1915 and Christmas 1917 she never saw or heard from him although he had been on leave in Bedford. On 7 October 1918 he wrote saying he would never make a joint home with her; during his stay in Canada he had met a lady with whom he fell in love and lived with her as her husband. He asked her not to write again as this was his final decision. On October 24th she saw him at the Cannon-street Hotel, London, and discussed business in connection with her hotel, and made a last appeal to him to come back to her.

These statements, made to the court to support her petition, particularly the last one about a last appeal to come back to her, are plainly not true. The love letters also give details of some of Bertie's visits to the Sow and Pigs – but the pair must have agreed to end the marriage in the quickest way possible.

We know from the love letters that during his time in Canada before the war, Bertie had met another woman. It seems that at the end of the war he was prepared to behave like a gentleman and take full blame for the failure of the marriage, thus allowing his wife to divorce him so that she could marry her lover. Of course, this also left him free to return to Canada and remarry.

At the end of this hearing in May the judge granted a decree nisi with costs, and the decree absolute for the dissolution of her marriage to Bertie was granted in the High Court on 10 November 1919.

Helen and Frank's wedding took place at Kensington Register Office seventeen days later, on 27 November 1919. This was a rather glamorous place for a divorcee to get married, and the two witnesses to the ceremony fitted the bill. They were Arthur William Godwin from the Royal Flying Corps and Edgar W. Hylton, also RFC but described as an actor. He appeared in a British Lion film production called *The Secret of the Moor* in 1919.

Helen described herself as Helen Armstrong, formerly Nelson, spinster, on her wedding certificate. She said she was previously the wife of Benjamin Bertie MacVicar Armstrong, from whom she obtained a divorce. There was no mention of the fact that she had earlier been married to

Helen's third marriage certificate, in which her first marriage to Edward Randell seems to have been erased, although she records her very recent divorce from Bertie under 'condition'. Curiously, she describes her father's profession as a farmer, although he was a retired policeman and a publican who was keeping chickens in the back garden of the King William IV when he died.

Edward Randell, perhaps avoiding any awkward questions as to the legal status of that marriage. Officially, Edward was classed as 'disappeared' rather than dead and so, technically, Helen had not been free to marry either Bertie or Frank.

Interestingly, according to the marriage certificate, although the drinks license of the Sow and Pigs was not officially transferred to a new publican until the following year, Helen appears to have finally broken free of the hotel. She gave her address as Elmtrees, Mollington, near Chester, where a new chapter of her life was to begin.

James Franklin-Smith, aged 35, is described as a bachelor and Lt-Col in the reserve of officers, and his address is given as South Kensington Hotel, Queens Gate, in London. This is the first time he calls himself James Franklin-Smith.

Considering there are so few facts given on a wedding certificate, it is remarkable how many on this one appear to be not quite right. Helen's age is given as 38, three years older than her husband, when she is in fact 39, and her father, who was variously a policeman and a publican, has become a farmer.

Yet finally, after six extraordinary years, Helen had got her man and she was no doubt ready to settle down to the life she had dreamed of and outlined in their love letters.

Bertie meanwhile, like Helen's first husband Edward, disappeared from her life. He returned to Canada, but in 1920 he was back in Europe, joining the Royal Ulster Constabulary. He married again and had two sons in Cornwall before taking his family to Canada permanently.

6

HAPPILY MARRIED AT LAST

As we have already noted from the love letters, Helen's dream was to leave the Sow and Pigs Hotel, marry Frank, and have his children. Already aged 39 when she married for the third time and not having had a child since Bob when she was 20, it might not have seemed as straightforward the second time around.

Helen, however, was full of surprises. In the summer of 1920 she gave birth to a daughter, Sheila Franklin-Smith, and three years later to a son, Hugh Norbury Franklin-Smith.

By this time Helen was 43 and Bob was 23. What happened to Bob and where she lived after she left her boarding school in Bedford was at first a mystery. By the time Frank and Helen were married she was 19, so she could already have started an independent life of her own. Her disappearance from the story was partly resolved when researchers contacted Helen's descendants and discovered they knew of a mysterious great-aunt called 'Bob' who lived in Germany. The younger members of the family had always been told that Bob was Helen's younger sister, and did not know she was her daughter – although clearly Frank must have known their true relationship. In later life she admitted Bob was in fact her daughter and half-sister to Sheila and Hugh.

Yet while Helen had achieved her dream of becoming Frank's wife and having his children, the family's finances appeared to be shaky. Frank, who

A portrait of James Franklin-Smith, known as 'Frank' to Helen. The
picture was among her papers but the date and location is unknown.

originally came from Manchester, had set Helen up in an egg farm at
Moston, near Chester. The Ministry of Defence encouraged a lot of ex-
soldiers to set up egg farms because at the end of the war food was still in
short supply. An investment in chickens to provide eggs must have seemed
a good choice. It also fulfilled Helen's long-held desire to get out of the
pub trade.

Frank had continued his career in the army and was quoted in the
Lancashire Daily Post of 25 September 1919, three months before his wedding to Helen, in his new role as officer in charge of the North Western
Directorate, whose mission was to find jobs for returning soldiers already
of good education when they joined the forces.

The paper reported an inaugural meeting held in Carlisle Town Hall of the 'interviewing committee' tasked with finding jobs in Cumberland and Westmorland for returning soldiers. The meeting was told that the organisation was to help men who volunteered at the beginning of the war who had either given up their education to enlist or already had qualifications. 'It was not concerned with men of inferior education,' the report said.

Owing to the difficulty of finding jobs, the committee was told that many of the best young men were emigrating to find work and the country was losing their talent. Lt-Col Franklin-Smith told the meeting that all members of his staff were men who had served on the front line and by wounds or illness had been rendered unfit for further active service.

The need for the department was shown by the fact that there were 25,000 men who wanted jobs. In Lancashire and Cheshire 4,000 cases had already been found jobs but in Westmorland and Cumberland between 300 and 400 were awaiting attention, and applications were coming in rapidly as the Army of Occupation was being demobilised.

Nearly a year later, on 12 August 1920, the *Manchester Guardian* interviewed Lt-Col Franklin-Smith under the headline 'Still Looking for Work – The delay in placing the demobilised'. He was quoted as saying that there was hardly a post that could not be filled by a capable ex-serviceman, yet this complex and widespread agency was not being used anything like as fully as it might be. He spoke of a man who had recently returned from Russia who found himself so destitute that he had to sleep in the Manchester workhouse. He spoke three languages – French, Russian and German – and was a shorthand typist and a bookkeeper, but was being forced to work as a porter from day to day to survive.

There were 'scores of other cases of quiet misery that could be relieved if employers would keep the Department of Labour Appointments aware of their needs'. He ended his interview with an appeal from the king to 'redeem a pledge to those who so nobly responded to the country's call. Let us hasten by common effort to discharge them, by securing suitable employment to every deserving ex-serviceman.'

Later still, in June 1921, continuing in his role as director of the service, Frank was writing to the *Lancashire Evening Post* saying that even though 5,000 ex-officers and rankers had been found jobs there were still 1,600 looking for work, many of whom had been unemployed for months:

They include a large proportion who are fitted for the positions of book-keepers clerks, or cashiers; there are others who are qualified for responsible positions in almost every trade and profession. I believe that everyone who succeeds in placing an ex-Service man in a situation will feel he has done something towards paying off a national debt.

However, while Frank was battling away on behalf of his unemployed comrades, something must have gone wrong with his own finances.

As far as the authors can tell from research, the family home was a house called Parkholm in the parish of Moston, in a rural area of Cheshire. It was a poultry and egg farm. Superficially, it would seem to have been a good business to be in because there was still a national shortage of food. It might also have been that feed was expensive for the same reasons and competition may have been fierce because too many ex-soldiers had invested in chicken farming to provide eggs. Either way, it was not possible for Helen to make the farm pay.

Frank appeared to have had a full-time job with the army while Helen was at that time looking after a toddler and running the egg farm. If that is correct, then she was certainly proving less succesful at managing a chicken farm than a hotel. All we know for sure is that from 1922–1928 she was registered as a voter at Parkholm and Frank as an absent voter. Frank could not have had much involvement because of his job. He travelled a great deal in the north west of England to various offices, of which he was the director. That is presumably why, as a serving soldier, he was registered for a postal vote.

On 24 May 1922, without any formal explanation, Frank resigned his prestigious job as director of the government's soldiers' employment agency. A week later, on 2 June, a notice appeared in the *London Gazette* stating that James Franklin-Smith, of Parkholm, a retired Lt-Col, had been made bankrupt.

This must have caused a serious crisis in the family, and for Helen, who had already had one husband declared bankrupt, it must have been doubly difficult, especially as this time she must have been at least partly responsible.

Although we do not have any details of the problems the family faced, it did not appear to have had a detrimental effect on their relationship. Their first child had been born and a second would arrive the following year.

Although the couple continued to live at Parkholm, Sheila was at St Ronan's boarding school in Duffield, Derbyshire. There are newspaper reports of her winning egg and spoon races on sports day in 1934, taking a leading part in the school play, *A Midsummer Night's Dream* by Shakespeare in 1935 and playing hockey for the school and lacrosse for the Derbyshire county schools first eleven in 1937.

Whatever else happened in their lives at Moston is not known, but the oral history of the family is that despite the bankruptcy in 1922 the retired Lt-Col started up the egg farm again. It is clear, however, that by September 1934 someone else had moved into Parkholm and the couple had returned to the pub trade in the West Country.

Exactly where their first venture together into the pub trade took place is not known, but family members believe it was a hotel at or near Exford, a village on Exmoor.

But by September 1938 they had moved again and this time found a permanent home at the Red Lion Hotel, at Wareham, Dorset. An inventory made out to James Norbury Franklin-Smith dated 15 September that year details furniture and fittings for the hotel worth £1,412 and stock in trade of £173 4s 5d. It was an enormous former coaching inn and a considerable undertaking for the family. The family – sometimes including the now-grown-up children, ran the Red Lion Hotel in North Street, throughout the Second World War and beyond.

One apparently unrelated but fascinating document that came to light during the authors' research, dated 28 May 1949, was from the High Court in London, the Principal Probate Registry. It reads: 'Be it known that Edward Randell of The Empire Theatre, Dover, Kent, died on or since the 23rd day of January 1900, the place of death being unknown, intestate.' In other words he did not leave a will. The document goes on: 'And be it further known that at the date hereunder written Letters of Administration of all the Estate which by law devolves to and vests in the personal representative [of Edward Randell ...] were granted to Helen Franklin-Smith of the Red Lion Hotel, Dorsetshire, married woman, the lawful relict of the said intestate.'

There is a certified statement at the bottom of the document saying that Edward Randell's estate was worth £591 1s 9d and that £16 12s 1d estate duty has been paid to the Inland Revenue.

A postcard produced by Helen and Frank to advertise the Red Lion Hotel at 1 North Street, Wareham. They took over the establishment just before the Second World War.

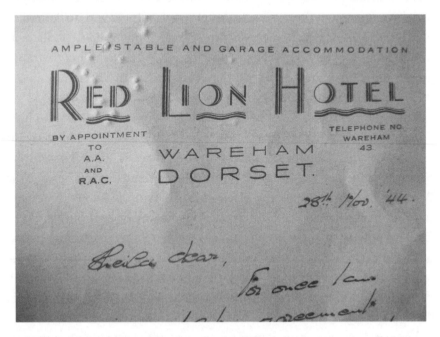

Red Lion Hotel notepaper, advertising both stables and garage accommodation. This letter, sent at the end of the Second World War, was written by Helen to her daughter Sheila. Her handwriting hardly changed since the love letters to Frank twenty-eight years previously.

In His Majesty's High Court of Justice.

The Principal Probate Registry.

BE IT KNOWN that *Edward Randell of The Empire Theatre Dover Kent*

died on or since ~~on~~ the *23rd* day of *January* 1900 *the place of death being unknown*

Intestate

AND BE IT FURTHER KNOWN that at the date hereunder written Letters of Administration of all the Estate which by law devolves to and vests in the personal representative of the said Intestate were granted by His Majesty's High Court of Justice at the Principal Probate Registry thereof to *Helen Franklin — Smith of The Red Lion Hotel Wareham Dorsetshire married woman the lawful relict of the said intestate*

And it is hereby certified that an Affidavit for Inland Revenue has been delivered wherein it is shewn that the gross value of the said Estate in ~~Great Britain~~ the *United Kingdom* (exclusive of what the said deceased may have been possessed of or entitled to as a Trustee and not beneficially) amounts to £ *597 — 1 — 9* and that the net value of the estate amounts to £ *597 — 1 — 9*

And it is further certified that it appears by a Receipt signed by an Inland Revenue Officer on the said Affidavit that £ *16 — 12* on account of Estate Duty and Interest on such duty has been paid,

Dated the *28th* day of *May* 19 *49*

Registrars Order dated the 20th day of November 1948

C.H. ——
Registrar.

Extracted by *Lacey and Son*

The High Court document that allows Helen to claim the money from the estate of her first husband, Edward Randell, which was left over after his bankruptcy was settled half a century earlier. Presumably the last time Helen saw him was on 23 January 1900, but this document shows that he was not officially declared dead until 28 May 1949 – nearly fifty years later. Legally, Helen could not remarry unless she could prove Edward was dead, although there is no evidence she attempted to do so. According to the hearings at the bankruptcy courts in Dover in the early 1900s, Edward had absconded and probably sailed to South Africa, leaving behind a pile of unpaid debts. There was no suggestion at any of the hearings that he had died.

A portrait of Sheila, Helen's daughter. We do not have a picture of Helen in her younger years but family members say that mother and daughter looked very much alike.

So, almost fifty years after she was deserted as a newlywed by her first husband, Helen made this application to have Edward formally declared dead. By doing so she inherited what was left of his fortune, decades after all his debts had been paid and his bankruptcy case closed by the Official Receiver. What prompted her after this long passage of time to have the Dover Millionaire declared dead is not known. As far as we can tell no trace of him had been found since he disappeared, and he had probably been long forgotten by all but Helen. However, if he had run away to South Africa, assumed another identity and led a different life, he could still have been alive in 1949. He would have been 70.

As it is, the court does not appear to have asked any searching questions, nor concerned itself with the fact that while her husband was legally still alive Helen had been married twice more. If they had, they might have discovered that the first of these marriages – to Bertie – took place quite soon after Edward disappeared and while the courts in Dover still regarded him simply as having absconded rather than missing presumed dead.

As we have seen, depending on the circumstances, in the early 1900s Helen variously described herself as a married woman and then a widow. It is doubtful that she knew for certain whether Edward was dead or alive, but

The Red Lion at Wareham was still a twelve-bedroom hotel in 2018. The front entrance is unchanged since Helen was the landlady during the Second World War. (*photo: Chris Goddard*)

The interior of the Red Lion in 2018. (*photo: Chris Goddard*)

she obviously concluded that whatever had happened to him she needed to get on with her life, and she did.

However, fifty years later Helen was prepared to risk some awkward questions about her past by applying to the High Court to have Edward declared dead. She might have been spurred on by the urgent need for some extra funds. Family members recall that Helen was a 'demon on the horses'. She had shelves at the Red Lion full of formbooks for racehorses. A family legend is that she once backed a Derby winner at 33 to 1.

On 14 January 1953, four years after the High Court in London formally declared her first husband dead, the love of Helen's life and third husband, James Norbury Franklin-Smith, landlord of the Red Lion Hotel in Wareham, died aged 71.

He was apparently a well-liked man and died of a heart attack while doing his daily accounts in his study, as he did every night at closing time. He left an estate of only £9 12s 6d, revealing that the family finances may not have been in good shape.

Helen, already 74, gave up the hotel trade later that year. The final inventory dated 1 September 1953 for the Red Lion said the value of furnishings and equipment was £2,769 1s 6d and the stock was worth £378. After paying all the relevant fees, Helen received a cheque for £2,230 19s 9d.

She moved to Market Harborough in Leicestershire, bought a house, and lived with her married daughter, Sheila Queen, her son-in-law and her grandchild, Tracey.

Tracey, who was a young child at the time, remembers granny studying the form in her father's daily newspaper and him complaining that his mother-in-law never folded the paper neatly afterwards. Helen was still betting on the horses. Sadly, she suffered from rheumatoid arthritis, a painful condition. She died on 27 November 1961, aged 82.

The twists and turns in Helen's remarkable life raise many questions that only she could have answered. Those that remember her in her later years when she was running the Red Lion described her as a strong-minded woman, sometimes 'ferocious', who 'ruled the roost', but that her husband James was always 'the governor'.

They had an extraordinary courtship that endured from 1913 and through the tribulations of the First World War until they were married in 1919. They then remained together for thirty-four years, until death parted them.

Helen, aged about 80, outside her home in Market Harborough, where she retired after Frank died.

Helen Franklin-Smith with her granddaughter Tracey Queen, taken in Market Harborough.

7

THE LOVE LETTERS

The letters are printed in chronological order, although it is possible that some are missing, lost through enemy action. Both Helen and Frank feared that some letters were being lost in the post on their tortuous journey between Toddington in Bedfordshire and Frank's army tent somewhere near Salonika in Greece. They took to numbering their letters to check whether they were all arriving, and some numbers are missing. This might simply be, as Helen sometimes admits, that she forgot to number some or that she got the sequence wrong, or it may be because some of the ships carrying the letters failed to reach their destination. Quite a few ships were sunk in the Mediterranean during this period. Also, some letters bear the same date, which either means Helen wrote two in a day, or that she made a mistake.

There are also two letters from Frank. How they got in the mix is not clear. The letters were deposited in a branch of Lloyds Bank in London during the First World War by a Mr Smith. This is presumably Captain Franklin Smith when he was home on leave. He married Helen but never returned to claim the letters.

5 September 1915

Frank, my husband,

So now sweetheart you are really out there, and I have said good bye to you and kissed you for the last time until you come back again – it has all been very dreadful, don't you think, Frank? I mean dear, your going away. Thank you so much for all your letters, particularly so this last week they have indeed been a comfort to me, I did not get a letter you know on Thursday and then [on] Friday of course I went to Bedford but the whole of the time I was there I just thought of you and your letter that would be waiting for me when I got home. All day yesterday I felt so very anxious, I do not know quite why but I could not keep my eyes off the clock. I think perhaps it was knowing you had left Aldershot and not being quite sure as to where you were, and then this morning immediately I was out of bed your dear telegram came, thank you so much my darling, I was so glad to get it and to know sweetheart [that] even at almost the last moment before you left England I was in your thoughts.

Frank dear, about your breeches, of course they are still here. I understand you to say darling that you will send a note for me to enclose with them but perhaps you did not have time last week, but will you please do so by return, kid, and tomorrow I will pack them up and return them to the people who made them as I find their name and addresses inside the breeches, and in your own note to them say you are writing to them in reference to the breeches that have been returned to them, please do not forget darling to do this.

I received the little key of the Despatch Box, but not the Bankers Receipt. You said you were enclosing it in your letter darling.

You have not told me how you managed to break the glass belonging to the silver case, tell me Frank have I to send you another? I love you my own darling husband, thank God the first Sunday will soon be over, the first Sunday nearer to seeing you again, write to me please, I am awfully anxious to get your first letter from France. I wonder which day it will arrive? I want you Frank darling, my own sweetheart.

Your wife Nell

7 September 1915

Frank, my darling,

I got a letter from you yesterday morning, was it not jolly nice kid? I was so glad it was the last letter from Aldershot, the one you wrote at 2am, Saturday morning you darling Frank – you did send me some topping letters last week, thank you so much, but you know how much your letters mean to me so you will understand just how I feel about them, but to get a letter from you on Monday morning knowing you were in France was more than I expected and I loved it. I was not out of bed when Mrs Bonner brought me the letter. I read it and just cuddled it up to me right inside my nighty, put it just where I used to love your hand, the hand with my two rings, and then I thought of you and loved you. If you could only have known exactly how much I loved you just then last Monday morning at about 7.50 you would, I am sure Frank dear, have been almost happy. I wonder what you were really doing at that time. And I do hope you got some sleep Sunday night, you must have had a very trying time last week Frank dear.

Your stuff arrived yesterday kid. Rose and I had quite a lot of fun trying to get the uniform case upstairs – what a huge thing it is, first the confounded thing got on to her feet and then on to mine and after all we had to fetch little Jack from the garden to help us. I have not really had time to decide where your clothes etc. shall be kept, but when I have unpacked and separated them I shall be able to decide better, but no doubt my darling the bulk of it in your own bedroom, but I really do begin to wonder what you have done with poor old Cross's book but perhaps I shall find it amongst your clothes – I hope so.

Darling, you said you would let me have your wrist watch [sic] – you have not done so. Please send it to me Frank. I want it. Goodbye my sweetheart, I love you, write to me. All my love is yours my darling.

Your wife, Nell
P.S. Re. my previous letter, of course I got the Bankers Receipt in your letter Monday morning.

9 September 1915

Frank, my own darling,

I got your little note yesterday, the one posted Sunday last, I was awfully
pleased to get it and to know you had really thought of me even as you
were going over to France – I am returning the envelope to you Frank
dear because I want you to see exactly how it arrived here quite open, of
course I agree the Censor man(?) opening the letter if he felt so inclined
but all the same I think it hardly the thing that should be sent onto me
not stuck in anyway, tell me darling, what did you write just underneath
your name, and why has that been crossed out? I am sending this letter to
you registered because I want you to tell me all about it, take this censor's
number and if you strike the gentleman please speak very seriously to him
on the matter.

I was awfully miserable last night kid. I do not quite know what made
me feel so depressed but I started unpacking your stuff yesterday and
I think that was really the start of it, but I shall not have to give way to
fits of miserable [sic] Frank. I quite understand I shall have to make the
best of it but there are and will be times when I shall want to be near you
if only just to touch you, and stroke your hair. I feel very unhappy Frank
dear – you understand that I do, do you not, kid?

I found Dr Cross's book, dear, amongst your things and there is a case
with knives and forks etc. – six pieces with pieces of cutlery missing and
I do not think they are yours kid, at least they do not bear your initials;
the initials appear to be J.P. Tell me Frank about them, do they belong
to you?

The photographs have not come yet – are they not a long time? I do
want them.

I am so anxious to get your next letters, are you feeling quite well?
I hope you are. I love you my husband. All my love is yours.

Always your very own, Nell

Saturday, 11 September 1915

Frank, my own darling,

Please write to me. I did expect a letter from you today. I thought as it did not come this morning it would certainly be here this afternoon but it has not come – has there not been time, kid, for a letter from you? I do not understand, but I do know that I have had two letters from Bertie this week, one dated last Monday the 6th and one the 7th.

Sunday, 12 September 1915

Darling, I am so sorry I did not finish this letter to you yesterday. I felt too jolly miserable kid, so I gave it up and even today, Frank, there is no letter from you, but perhaps tomorrow – I shall so soon get anxious if I do not hear from you because I love you so very much Frank and I miss you frightfully, particularly so at the weekends and you have been really out there a week; of course, dear, I quite understand that for the first day or two you would find quite a lot to do, at least I should think you would and perhaps that accounts for me not getting a letter.

Have you missed me very much sweetheart since a fortnight today? I was very unhappy last night after I got up to bed. I cried about you quite a lot the whole evening, was very depressing [sic], and when I go into the billiard room [on] Saturday evenings I miss you, the room seems somehow wrong without you – once or twice, perhaps you do not remember, when I have been coming down stairs I have looked up and I have just caught your eyes – I mean through the banisters rails from the billiard room – and I have loved you frightfully just then and have felt so jolly happy. Do you remember, Frank, how I mean? I hope you do.

You love me sweetheart, do you not? I know you do but please write and tell me you do. I want so badly to be told, and I think loved for just a tiny minute today, but after I get your letter I shall feel better about everything – I am quite sure I shall.

Frank my husband, goodbye.

Always your very own, Nell

15 September 1915

Frank, my dearest,

Thank you so much for your topping letters. I have had three this week. Forgive me, Frank, for being so anxious about not hearing from you in my last letter but I felt, kid, that I could not go on unless I heard from you very soon. I am going to Bedford Monday next to take the kid back to school so I will get the things you ask for and post them to you Tuesday darling.

Your Jig Saw [sic] Puzzle, you would have been frightfully amused if you could have seen Bob and I with her atlas. Bob was lying full length on her tummy on her side of the bed and I was kneeling by the side. Frank dear, Amiens is it not? I am still not quite clear, tell me, but you do know how really dense I am and stupid do you not, but then dear at times you write so badly – please return the enclosed slip with explanation.

Your photographs came yesterday but I have returned the ½ dozen sitting positions they had (after all your written instructions) vignetted them almost smaller than those from Kinghams. I do not know what they will say and I care less – you quite agree with me in returning them do you not? I did not like them, they were not at all as we wished.

So you have missed me just a tiny bit my husband since you have been away. I am so glad, so glad my darling, you have said in two of your letters about when I meet you when you return to England – you do mean that, Frank, do you not? I am to meet you really right off the boat, I mean.

The weather up to now has been perfect – such lovely days. I am awfully glad kid, as you say the sunshine is such a great help.

I have put one of your photographs in the silver frame. I mean the frame dear that once stood in your bedroom with my photograph – you remember darling, you once flung it into the grate [you] 'bad tempered swine', but your photograph looks jolly nice in it now.

Your letters have been very interesting Frank dear. I do wish I could be with you to watch the panorama because even just in the ordinary way there is quite a lot that appeals to us, is there not darling? I know of one thing in particular – 'guess'.

Goodbye my darling

I love you and will write to you again very soon.

Your wife, Nell

17 September 1915

My darling,

Frank dearest, I missed you so much yesterday, I think perhaps it was a tiny bit to do with your photograph. I looked at it many times and kissed it more times than I should care to admit to any living soul bar you, but I could tell you my darling, tell you just anything. I feel sure there would never be the tiniest thing I should want to keep away from you, I do not know why I should feel quite like this, only that I love you so absolutely, but before I met you even with Tommy there was always one or two things I did not want him to know, but with you my husband it is all so different, are you glad Frank? Or do you think I love you too much, no not too much do I, kid, and you are never going to be unkind to me again are you? I was just right down in the very depths of despair last night, please forgive me sweetheart, but you will quite understand how I felt kid, when I tell you that I thought all over again of the two horrible days I had in London when I was supposed to be there with you and I was equally as unhappy about the whole affair last night as I was when in London – is it not too horrible when one cannot forget, and I can't, I have never been able to since I was a tiny kid, but Frank dear at the same time I never bear real malice, but I do wish it had not happened, darling you too wish it had not happened, tell me. I suppose more or less it was an eye opener for me with all the men I had previously been out with, I had always been made so much of and when you treated me so jolly unfairly I could not understand, neither have I been able to since, but you did promise you would never be unkind to me again, but tell me in your next letter.

    I am messy today, but not as bad as yesterday. Heaven alone knows how I am going to get through the long dreary Winter <u>**without you**</u>, I hate and detest the thought of staying on here, this house I am sure will make me quite old and then you will not love me, Frank, I am quite sure you will not.

    Yesterday and today are two perfect days but very hot, and yesterday evening was perfect. I did so want you to be here so that we could have toddled into the Garden together, the Sweet Peas have been and are still very lovely.

I do not think I told you that another canvas package arrived for you some days after the first three. I think perhaps it is your camp bedstead, but the label does not appear to be in your writing. I am enclosing the label.

My darling, thank you so much for your kind enquiries after Bob. I cannot quite remember if I told you I had arranged for her to go to Howard College; when I went there, I found the place to all appearances quite nice, and I think Miss Smith the Principal would be nice to live with and at the same time thorough. Sweetheart I love you, you know I do, I am just living and waiting for you to come back to me.

Always your own, Nell

19 September 1915

Frank, my own darling,

I shall be away from home tomorrow so sweetheart I am going to write just a short letter to you today. I have been busy this morning packing Bob's clothes as I think I told you before kid, I take her down to school tomorrow. Three weeks this evening since I last saw you, the time to me has gone very very slowly, it seems months instead of weeks but thank God one more week end nearly over, one week end [sic] nearer to the time when I shall meet you at Folkestone – will it not be just perfect when I do meet you? And Frank I shall want to kiss you awfully badly immediately I see you, but I suppose you would think it frightfully unsoldierly to kiss me with other people looking on, but I should not care a damn – you will have to look jolly smart if I do not.

Dr Cross came in yesterday – he told me that he is leaving Toddington in a fortnight, he has got a commission, he seemed awfully pleased about it, he is going to pay me a special visit before he goes away as I told him I do so want to see him in khaki.

Darling, I do hope you will not mind waiting a few days for the things you asked me to send out to you. I thought, dear, as I was going down to Bedford tomorrow Monday, I could get your hankies and send them all at the same time and Frank, my darling, do not forget to tell me should there be anything else you want and will you let me know when you want more Tobacco and Cigarettes or have I to send a certain quantity regularly? I forget if we arranged about this.

I think I told you before your letters are interesting and I love them, please keep on writing to me. I have somehow got mixed up in timing over this notepaper but you will understand. I am quite well, Frank dear, my cold was a perfect beast to get rid of but at last I have managed it, are you keeping well dear?
All my love dearest,

Your wife, Nell

Tuesday, 21 September 1915

My own darling,

I am afraid I shall not have time for a very long letter today, dear, your parcel seems to have taken me such a long time to pack but I hope it will arrive safely, darling, please let me know when it reaches you. Frank, dear, you will notice I have sent on the same photographs that I spoke to you about in a previous letter. I understand from Thomson's that they were obliged to vignette them to finish them as Scetch [sic] Portraits. I do not know if I can make it quite clear to you, but to leave the whole thing as the proof, the photograph would have to be finished and stuck on to a card, so I have asked them to do two this way, the Assistant thought I should not really care for them stuck on as it is a white background, but at the same time she was not at all keen I should have the half dozen Scetch [sic] Portraits unless I liked them, but I think they will do, it was two of each position you wished me to send out was it not? Of course, darling, if you want any more you must write to me.

Sweetheart, do you not think I am awfully good in sending you the card boards, string and brown paper for you to post them back to your own people in, or do you think I ought to have been an **Old Maid** in being so fussy, tell me please, give me your candid opinion as to this.

About your hankies, darling, you did not say if you wished for the light or the dark shade in khaki – if you prefer the lighter shade return those

I have sent and I will exchange them. I think they are rather nice and the quality not at all bad for half a crown each.

Bob went off quite alright to school yesterday. She claimed two of your photographs – she says you told her she might have two so when we were in Bedford she asked me to buy her a frame for one of them, and of course the one she preferred was 6/6d and I could not talk her into caring for either of the other frames, so of course it meant six shillings and sixpence. I do not know if the confounded photograph is really worth it.

I dare not write any more today, sweetheart; this letter is now much longer than I intended it to be, but then it is to you and it makes all the difference in the world because I love you and love writing to you my husband. Goodbye dearest.

Always your very own, Nell

24 September 1915

Frank, my own darling,

A week tomorrow since I last heard from you. Frank, Frank dear, do you understand what it means to me not hearing from you? Of course you understand. I am sorry in a way that I have not written to you for six days but I could not help it, for the life of me kid I could not write. I have just waited day after day for the post, every day with the same result, no letter.

In my last letter to you I talked of sending your tobacco and cigarettes as this week, but I have not sent them. I do not really know why but several times Mrs Bonner has spoken of you coming home and that perhaps you would be here for Christmas. I do not think I have quite thought so but perhaps once or twice I have, but today is the 24th, Christmas Eve, and I have not heard.

My God, Frank, I could not explain to you how I feel about everything but I think I am the unhappiest woman in the whole world. Christmas 1915, how I hate the thoughts of it. I shall be glad when it is all over and the New Year started, the year of 1916, my year, Frank dear, and not under any circumstances will I be here for the Christmas 12 months from now. I love you Frank my husband, you know I do, but not even if you ask me will I stay here very much longer, I shall just do as I have done before, take my chance with equally as much result I suppose, no great things. I have not heard from Bertie since he left here Dec 2nd, neither do I want [to]. I hate everybody that comes in here, particularly so during the last fortnight, and I want to get away from here so badly.

Frank dearest what is the matter? Why do I not get your letters? I cannot understand, but one thing I feel sure of [is] that whatever happens you will always love me and that you will never give me up, I do really feel so, although at times I am miserable and imagine all sorts of things and now that I am not getting your letters it is so easy to get despondent and troubled, but perhaps soon I may have a letter and then everything will seem lighter. Goodbye my dearest one, and please forgive me if my letters are miserable. I love you so much and always want you.

Your wife, Nell

24 September 1915

You have not sent me the letter for the people that made your breeches – have you sent direct to them? Tell me and please do not neglect to do so. I mean write to them on the matter. I told them you would do so.

Frank, my own darling,

I have had two topping letters from you, one yesterday and one today, thank you so much, they have made me feel almost happy. I say almost, sweetheart, because, Frank, I am more than sure I shall never be really happy until I am married to you – pray God it may be very soon.

I have had a most dreadful fright re. enclosed miniature, I really wanted to cut it the exact size for your case, I have taken off a tiny bit each side but I had a most difficult job in cutting it. I began to think I should make a mess of the whole thing so I dare not touch it again. Frank, if it is still a tiny bit too large you will want something very sharp to cut it with and now my darling do you like it? I think I do. I shall be awfully anxious to hear what you have to say about it.

Sweetheart please help me to decide. I want to buy a frame for your second photograph, I do not know which to have. I am enclosing you several sketches of frames taken from Vickery's Catalogue. I do not understand it, have the East Lancashire a Regimental Colour? Because by the sketch I rather like No. X3000 No. 3, in your reply dear please tell me about which Badge, also the Colours. I have marked the frames and please do not forget to turn over the page. I say, kid, I have just thought of something – do you remember one night in bed when I kept on making you turn over? From what I can remember you were rather grumpy at being disturbed. I wonder, darling, if it were possible and if under the same circumstances you would grumble tonight, no a thousand times no, ay kid? Because for a very long time you would be kept busy, sleep would be out of the question. Frank, in a way I hate to think of it and at the same time to know that I cannot even be near you if only just to touch you.

Please do not forget to return sketches of frames by return post.

My darling, yes, I am awfully glad I have got your photographs, frightfully pleased kid, please whisper it Frank, but every night up to now I have kissed it before getting into bed just when I am in my nighty all ready for bed. I take it down from the shelf and usually kneel by the side of my bed and look at it for quite a long time and then kiss it and then into bed, if I have had a letter from you through the day I always read it (for the last time that day) after I am in bed and then lie and think about you. Sometimes I am almost happy, sometimes utterly miserable, but you understand do you not my husband I love you so much and after I have been in bed for quite a long time and the room dark, the stars just peeping out, I whisper, Frank dear, there are thousands and thousands of our men out at the War but very few my darling that are loved and thought of, I love and think of you. I am sure of this Frank, I love you in a way that comes to very few women through their lives and I am glad, my husband, I would not have it otherwise.

Dearest goodbye,

Always your own, Nell

26 September 1915

Frank, my own darling,

Sunday afternoon, I do not think I shall be able to finish this letter in time for the post today because I have been resting. I hate Saturdays and Sundays, Frank, without you and I never seem to get a letter from you Sunday mornings, I wish I did. I wonder if you have got your parcel that I posted to you Tuesday last? I should think perhaps by now you have, I am quite anxious to know if it reaches you in good condition as one reads of so many parcels getting broken and lost.

My sweetheart, you ask[ed] me in your last letter if I remembered Christmas two years ago, yes Frank I do remember every tiny little thing about it. I did not want you to go away, not even then, do you remember how it kept on getting later and later – Christmas Eve before you dragged yourself away, I was awfully happy, no, I am not likely to forget, I felt much too ghastly. Tell me, do you remember who the particular person was that had made me feel so jolly ill? Then on Christmas Day I had my letter, my very own letter, the one you always swore you would never write to me and then Boxing Day, dear, you came back to me wearing your green woolly waistcoat and I had been so jolly poorly. Frank, I wonder if you really do remember all this?

Before I forget kid, in one of your letters you said do you think it quite fair to throw B.B.M.A. correspondence in my face, you were a beast Frank to suggest that I had done so – how could I, darling, when I hate and detest his letters. I feel very troubled when I think that perhaps very soon he may be coming home, I do not know what I shall do but one thing I am certain about I shall feel pretty desperate. I felt bad enough about things when he returned from Canada, but now, Frank, to me everything seems different, I feel altogether more sure of you and when he came home just over twelve months ago I do not think I had quite made up my mind about you kid, not really, I do not think, but I am quite certain now, quite sure that I love you more than anything else in the world and nobody, not even Tommy, will ever be able to take me away from you.

I say Tommy, Frank dear, because I really used to think before I met you my husband that I had loved him, but I could not have done so could I, Frank? But in a way I am fond of him now, but I love you kid, I know

I do – I have never felt about anyone else as I feel about you. I am sure absolutely certain, I worship you, you are everything in the world to me. I am a tiny bit sorry now I have mentioned Tommy, but you will not mind dear, will you? You will quite understand and are not jealous are you, Frank?

Forgive me kid, but you will not forget about my cheque quite early in October, how much did you owe me? I forget, you have insisted on me staying here but I am quite sure I do not know how I am going to pay through the Winter, even now I am troubled, but I will not worry about it anymore than I can possibly help. Write and tell me you love me and that you still want me to live here. Goodbye my dearest,

Your wife, Nell

30 September 1915

Frank, my own darling,

I was not going to write to you until tomorrow but I have received a letter from you this afternoon complaining rather much about not hearing from me more often; Frank, I really have sent you numbers of letters since you have been out in France – nearly every other day, with one or two exceptions. This week is an exception because today is Thursday and the last letter I posted to you was last Sunday night at about nine o'clock, but when I explain to you that Bertie is home you will perhaps understand and at the same time I hope feel a tiny bit sorry for me.

When I last wrote to you, which of course was Sunday, I did not know he was on his way home – he arrived Sunday night after we were all in bed, coming off the late train at Luton and of course driving from there, he is home to take his Commission and goes to Curragh Camp Ireland Wednesday next with the Reserve Squadron 2nd King Edwards Horse.

It was strange, Frank darling, was it not that I should have spoken in my last letter about him coming home. I cannot write anymore tonight but tomorrow dear I will write you again. I love you my husband, love you all the more through him coming home, but I am miserable kid and very unhappy. Goodbye Frank, please write to me. I feel sure I need not tell you that nothing has happened but this time he is not so easily put off, truly I cannot quite understand his intention, he speaks of seeing Durance and winding up the whole affair, it is immaterial to me, he must please himself.

All my love dearest,

Your very own wife, Nell

1 October 1915

Frank, my own darling,

By now dearest no doubt you have got my miniature. I wonder if you like it? Bertie has gone down to Bedford so I want to get this letter finished before he comes back. I feel a tiny bit more settled this morning but during the last four days I have really wondered if life is worth living, if the whole thing in the finish will be worth [it], will ever be able to repay me for what I am going through now, but Frank dear I have never really thought that my luck is quite out, because last Sunday night I did not hear the conveyance stop. Mrs Bonner came down to my room and asked for the key, I asked her what she wanted it for and she replied for Mr Armstrong. I was very sleepy, I remember saying which Mr Armstrong, she said Mr Bertie. I simply said has he got home then? I did not even get out of bed, but immediately after she had gone from my room I thought what real luck you were not here because I felt very sure if you had been here you would have been in my bed because you know, darling, I could never keep you out in the ordinary way, could I? I have thought about it once or twice, kid, and have felt rather amused, but at the same time I am unhappy, Frank, but thank God I have quite a big sense of humour and as the thing might have been, seemed funny to me.

I am expecting your socks, kid, and will send them with your cigarettes and tobacco, probably on Monday. Today is Friday and I have told you once or twice if there is anything else you want let me know and I will, if at all possible, send it out to you. I did not manage to finish this letter this morning and the Postman has just been. There is a letter from you saying you have got the miniature and that you like it awfully, I am ever so glad

Frank, I too thought it was rather nice my darling. Don't you remember it was done from one of the photographs you returned to me, the one I wired for – no, I am quite sure I have not had it taken again (too damned badly off), but it certainly was the photograph I always thought the best, I just took the beads and earrings down in my little bag.

Re. what did I scratch out, please mind your own business and do not be so inquisitive, my memory fails me but I believe I have told you this before.

Please keep on loving me because I always want you to love me, and write to me very often.

Your wife, Nell

2 October 1915

Frank, darling,

Please explain to me about the enclosed, <u>I believe</u> I have told you before that I cannot understand you and Frank, dear, I am quite certain you told me a long time ago that these people 'Reids' had been paid. I am sending them your address and will you please have the receited [sic] bill sent direct to me. As you will already know, I have been more than troubled these last few days and the enclosed arriving this afternoon will not improve this evening for me, and Saturday evening out of all nights in the week I hate. I have not time, or at least I am not in the mood to write a long letter today, but write to me please, and tell me.

Your own, Nell

Letter from Reid Brothers,
Tailors and Breeches Makers
Hunting, Sporting and Motoring Outfits
Service Kits a Speciality
Norfolk House
209 Oxford Street
London W

1st October 1915

Mrs Armstrong
Toddington
Dunstable

Madam,

You will remember some time ago you were good enough to introduce us to Mr Franklin Smith. As we are desirous of getting into communication with him, we should esteem it a favour if you would kindly forward us his present address, for which purpose we enclose stamped addressed envelope.

With compliments,
Yours faithfully,
REID BROS
Collection Department

5 October 1915

Nell, darling,

The less said about your letter received this morning the better. I did not know <u>Reids</u> still were unpaid – but a cheque goes to them today. The receipt shall be duly sent to you in pursuance of your ORDER.

My sympathy is entirely with the unfortunates who came in contact with you while you were in the mood which <u>made you</u> write to me as you did. Good bye

Yours ever, Frank
Frighfulness [sic] is the speciality of the Bosche.

5 October 1915

Frank, my own darling,

I am afraid you will think I have been a long time in sending out your things but the delay has really been caused in waiting for your socks and even now I am not sending them, at least not today. 3 pairs came up this morning from Harry Hills but they are much too large for you, I have been along to Dean's and they are expecting a fresh delivery of socks so I will send them immediately – I manage[d] to get three satisfactory pairs but there appears to be a great scarcity of woollen socks.

Bertie left here yesterday, I told you Wednesday in my letter but I had made a mistake, he went over to Ireland last night. Frank, you will have to forgive me if I cannot quite settle down just at present. I could not describe to anyone just how I have felt this last week, everybody coming in, and over from places round about to see him, and going away thinking he is more wonderful than ever when I know only too well how absolutely empty headed he is, shallow, just nothing below the surface, I am more mystified than before, however [sic] a level headed woman like myself came to marry a damned fool like him God only knows. It is too much for me, I have given it up.

Sweetheart, your letter of yesterday was somewhat a relief where you say this will be the second winter I shall be alone, but thank Heaven it will be the last. Yes, you are quite right, kid, it will indeed be the last, I shall not have time to explain to you in this letter but next week I am starting to pack quite a number of small things about the place that belong to me, you know, Frank, I have felt for a long time like deciding off on my own bat about getting out of the place and I think the horror of last week and then Reid's letter on top helped my decision quite finally.

I will tell you more in my letter tomorrow, so for the present my darling goodbye, even if you are a shit to me you know I love you.

Always your own, Nell

6 October 1915

Frank, my own darling,

Do you know, kid, I got your box packed yesterday with your British Warm, Cigarettes, Tobacco and Pumice Powder, also the Dermic Jellie and when I got into the Post Office the confounded thing weighed 12 lbs. I felt so sure I had got it under the 11 lbs but of course I had to bring it back and lighten the weight, so I am sending the Dermic Jellie in with your Rubber Boots. I may not send them today because I am waiting for the Carrier to see if he brings your socks, but in any case I will send your boots first post tomorrow morning.

Are you keeping quite well sweetheart? I trust you are – I am not feeling so well again this week, I suppose it is because of being so frightfully troubled the whole of last week. Frank, my darling, I wonder what you will say when you know I have quite decided to get out of the house in the early Spring, but I hardly know how to start getting ready or how to try to let the place for the best, can you advise me Frank dear? I wonder if you can, my idea is of packing up quite a lot of the small stuff into packing cases and then when Christmas is over send some of the best of the furniture with the cases to be stored at Bedford – of course there would not be very much furniture worth sending away – and then have an inventory taken and decide as to what price we can ask for the place, or can you suggest anything better? Of course in the way of packing the small stuff if will take me quite a number of weeks because I get such a small amount of spare time but I feel, Frank, it has got only to be done once and by so doing it will be making a start.

I will wait darling for your letter in reply to this and see what you have to say, but you do quite understand do you not that things cannot go on as they are, you do know what I mean, it is rather difficult to state things plainly in a letter but with you, my husband, I do not think it should be too difficult.

It is 2½ years since Bertie went to Canada and on my oath Frank not once since then have I been a wife to him, please tell me you believe me, you do believe me do you not? I often think about it myself and to me it seems almost an impossibility for anyone to believe. Frank, you do not know (if you did you would be frightfully sorry for me) how it has bothered me Bertie coming home again. I am sure I feel as most people must feel when they are just on the border of a nervous breakdown, forgive me, kid, but I almost feel that the whole thing is too much for me and that I cannot even now carry it through.

Frank, if you do love me as much as you have always said you do, for God's sake write to me and tell me again that you will never change your mind about wanting me when the War is over. You will be able to judge by this letter exactly how worked up I am and the only consolation I have is this sort of thing will age me years in appearance and for your sake, Frank, I do not want to look too old. You would not love me then, would you?

Today I am loving you again frightfully. Reid's letter made me feel for about two days not quite so sure of you, but I know you will explain to me all about it in your letter.

Goodbye my darling, I love you and want to be comforted so badly but only by you, nobody [else] in the whole world, only you.

Your wife, Nell

7 October 1915

Frank, my own darling,

I got your letter this morning, the one written last Sunday the 3rd, and I just feel as if I must sit down and write to you and tell you that since reading it in bed this morning I feel rather better about everything, thank you so much, Frank, for writing me such a topping letter because I really do want nice letters just now, but only from you, it is a great comfort to me to know my darling you are sorry for me. I explained to you in my letter of yesterday how truly unhappy I have been and how jolly ill it has made me feel. Honestly, Frank, it has taken it out of me this time more than before dear, but darling I love your letter and I feel sure tonight I shall sleep. Just lately I have had some very bad days but the nights, Frank, have been too dreadful.

I cannot quite think what made me lose faith in you, but night after night I have almost made myself believe that after the War perhaps you would change your mind, and then I used to lie in bed for hours and hours and wonder what I should do if after all you did not want me, but of course dear it was because I was bothered, terribly worried, but at the same time it is unfair to you to imagine for one moment you will ever tire of me and after reading your letter I feel now as I felt this morning, just relieved and I feel once again, my husband, that in your life I really do stand first.

I cannot write you any more tonight because dearest for eight days I have really done nothing but worry and now I must start work. I am anxious to get your letter re. the packing.
All my love, everything Frank

Your wife, Nell

Sunday, 10 October 1915

Frank, my own darling,

You did not love me, kid, did you when you wrote to me the enclosed. I do not like it so I am returning it to you, you have been unkind to me Frank.

Have you got both your parcels? I am really very sorry about the delay re. the second parcel, the one with your Rubber Boots, but I was kept waiting for the socks and even those I sent, Frank, I am not sure if you will like, they are quite the longest in the leg I can procure. I mean, dear, taking into consideration your size foot of course I can get socks quite long in the leg but with feet large enough for Bertie, then again I do not know if those sent will be warm enough. I was rather afraid to send pure wool socks because as a rule they shrink so frightfully, but Frank dear you must let me know if they are not quite what you want. Of course I could get them made for you, but let me know Frank and give me the length. About the Dermic Jellie, would you like some more sent out? I had no real idea how this stuff would be put up so I sent to Harrods for it and asked them to send about a lb, but I will send you some more immediately I hear from you, that is of course if you want it.

Now going back to your two letters received this morning. I do not like either really, one was written when you were quite cross with me and the other when you were fed up. You say you still want to know what it was that I scratched out at the top of page No. 3. I really do not remember; it may have been the same word written down twice because you know darling sometimes when I am writing to you I have to leave the letter quite a number of times. It really is a great wonder I do not make more mistakes than I do, but I am very anxious to know when I made the mistake you speak of, please tell me. I am referring to your letter where you say 'by the way when you are trying to be rude, do spell correctly'. Frank darling please send the letter to me, I will without fail return it to you. I am frightfully sorry sweetheart that I spell badly, please forgive me.

Thank you for the £10 cheque, also received this morning. How much did you really owe me? Please tell me, I would much rather know.

About your cigarette case, the large pigskin one that you got from Vickery's just before you left England. I thought I understood you to say it was quite a cheap one because, dear, my account came from there about two days ago and the cigarette case is entered at £1.2.6. Please let me know by return about this because if there is a mistake I must draw there [sic] attention to it at once.

My darling I must not write any more today, I am afraid of missing the post, but I will write you again tomorrow, my husband I love you, cheer up Frank, you were miserable.

With all my love dearest, I want you awfully badly to be here kid, want you in one or two different ways do you understand, Frank, do you know exactly what I mean?

Your wife, Nell

                                                      11 October 1915

Frank, my own dearest,

I got your letter this morning, the one written on the 7th where you accuse me of losing my temper. My darling I did not lose my temper and, Frank, I really do write to you quite a lot. I begin to think you cannot get all my letters. Of course, dear, I did not have very much opportunity to write to you when Bertie was here and even when I could have written I felt too jolly miserable.

About the letter I sent to you re. Reid's account (the letter that you call a thing) perhaps I am a tiny bit sorry, forgive me sweetheart, but you should have taken into consideration, Frank, that I was worried almost to death.

I am awfully glad you really do want my letters, and that they make a tiny bit of difference to you out there, and you say that you love me as I have never been loved in my life before. Thank you so much, Frank, and when we are married – because we are going to be married are we not? – you shall prove that all you have said to me in your letters is quite true, but I know it is true and I know you will be awfully good to me.

Seven weeks yesterday since I last said goodbye to you, six weeks since you left England. I wonder if another six weeks and all is well if I may then look forward to you coming home for a few days, when you are really coming home, Frank, I do not know quite what I shall do, probably go mad with excitement.

I miss you so much sometimes and there are days when I feel as if I cannot go on without you. Last evening being Sunday the house was quiet. I sat talking to Mrs Bonner and several others, I felt then, Frank, as if I wanted you so badly I just had to get up and walk through into the Commercial Room where the room was quite dark of course, but that did not matter. I sat on the table for a tiny minute and just whispered 'Frank, Frank darling'. If you could only have known sweetheart how much I was loving you just then you would have been happy, my husband, I feel sure you would. I thought about you such a lot yesterday, I think more than usual, although that wants a lot of beating, but I loved you awfully yesterday and after I got to sleep I dreampt [sic] of you, which is quite unusual for me – I so seldom dream of you, I wish I often could, but last night you were topping almost as nice as I have ever known you. I don't know, Frank, but I think I ought to see a Doctor.

Are you keeping quite well dearest? Tell me in your next letter, I am anxious about you. When I think of the dreadful winter coming on and your bad colds you always get. I hope you noticed your nice new button on your British Warm, I sent Rose specially into Dunstable for it (please say thank you Nell darling).

My own darling I love you, tell me dear if there is anything you want sent out. I asked you about the cigarette case in my letter yesterday, please do not forget to let me know at once.
My husband goodbye.

Always your very own, Nell

14 October 1915

Frank, my own darling,

I have not very much time this evening but as I may not have time to write to you tomorrow, I just want to send a tiny letter to you tonight.

I am thinking of going to Bedford tomorrow, I do not want to go, not really, but I promised the kid when she went back to school that I would come down one day and take her out to tea so tomorrow is the day. I shall think about you sweetheart and no doubt dear we shall talk of you quite a lot.

I am anxious, kid, about your British Warm which I posted to you on Tuesday October 5th, you have not mentioned it in either of your last letters, I trust by now darling you have received it, I feel sure the box had not reached you when you last wrote to me although it appears to me there had been ample time. I say I feel sure, Frank, because you are always most appreciative of every tiny thing that one does for you, it is just one of your nice ways, and this particular one I love, but you will let me know when you get the two parcels will you not, dear? Your Rubber Boots etc. I posted to you on Friday October 8th. I will write to you again on Saturday sweetheart, which will make five letters to you this week, not bad going, what say you kid?
Dearest, all my love always,

Your wife, Nell

16 October 1915

Frank, my own darling,

I have been to Bedford and quite enjoyed going. I found the kid awfully
well. I went down on the 11.51 train, did some shopping and then met her
at 3 o'clock. I took her back to the College at about 7.15 and came home by
the 8.14 train. I felt awfully fit yesterday and not the tiniest bit tired and
found upon reaching home a topping letter from you. Frank, thanks so
much dear, how strange, kid, that you should have said in this particular
letter of yesterday. (My wish has always been that I might be able to show
you how really grateful I am but I am afraid I have not always been able)
because dear if you have <u>kept</u> my letter that I posted to you Thursday
last, Oct 14th, you will see that I told you the day before I got your letter,
how really appreciative you always are and I trust, kid dear, you will
always be so and never get into that beastly way of taking everything for
granted. I think taking things for granted is a woman's privilege but never
a man's, a man must always ask very very nicely for everything he wants,
and once, only just once in a lifetime say '<u>May I?</u>'

You say, 'You are quite sure kid that you will not mind even if I am
crocked?' No, my husband, a thousand times no, of course I hope and
pray you will come back sound and well but if you are to be badly crocked
my darling then I hope your eyesight and your hands will be spared to
you because when we are married, Frank, we are going to have a real
piano and then nearly always when I ask you, you will play to me. I say
<u>nearly always</u> because if you remember quite a number of times when
I have asked you to play to me you have flatly refused to do so.

I was awfully amused re. your letter where you say 'tucked up in your
flannel nighty not one of the fancy ones'. Frank, how dare you, I am quite
sure both kinds are very nice – which do you like best, tell me.

You say that you want me to tell you that I love you, my God, Frank.
I do not think it is love, I cannot quite understand what it is, and you
must feel the same. You came to Toddington nearly 2½ years ago and
since then or nearly that amount of time I have been entirely in your
hands, loving you absolutely, just living for you, having no interest for
anyone else in the world only you, Frank, you do know only you are like
me, you always want to be told.

I often think about the first time I came to you, which must have been quite the end of October, then my condition a week or a fortnight before Christmas, and then again before Easter and several times since then, you need not ask me, need you my darling, facts along have proved to you how you are always just what I want.

I will write to you again dear very soon, my very own Frank are you not? And you are glad, quite glad!
Goodbye dearest,

Your wife, Nell

18 October 1915

Frank, my own darling,

I did not write to you yesterday, in the afternoon I rested a tiny bit and then did just a little writing, one letter to Bertie insisting on Reids bill being paid at once – the amount is £28.0.0 – and that the cheque for the same should be sent to me. I do not know how I shall get on – I may be told to mind my own business.

Yes, I do think you are unfair to want me to write so often, you are greedy Frank dear, but no letter tomorrow as I am going to be awfully busy, Wilkins is coming in to help me with the Harness Room, just the first start to the packing, kid, as I told you in a previous letter of mine that I get so little spare time because, darling, I always seem to be writing to you and I never seem to do any needlework and I have yards waiting to be done. I must really get up earlier in the mornings and not go to bed in the afternoons, but just those days when I do not write to you I hate it and often wish I had done so.

I had a very bad attack of the miserables [sic] last evening, it was too dreadful for words. I really did wonder again what I should do all through this long dreary Winter, I love you so much, kid, if I did not do so I would not stay on here, but of course I am going to at least for another six months, you did ask me to write and tell you what I thought of doing after I had left the house, I do not quite know darling but I would not decide on anything definite without asking you dear, you would rather I did this, would you not Frank?

Vickerys do not seem to think they have made a mistake, certainly their cigarette case at 4/6 is nothing like the cigarette cast that came here for you so I suppose the account will have to be left as it is, you do not remember do you sweetheart, just one of your mad days was it not?

Dearest, I will write to you again on Wednesday, I do wish you were coming home kid.

Always darling,

Your very own, Nell

France, 20 October 1915

I shall not be able to write you a long letter old girl, but I just feel I must write to you. It gives me quite a lot of pleasure to concentrate all my mind on you and say to you on paper what I am unable to say to you in person.

I told you that I thought we were about to move – I know now that we are going to, but exactly where or when I do not know yet. Pray God it is not to Serbia, although rumour seems to point that way. Please go on writing to me just the same, kid, because your letters will reach me wherever I am.

It is getting steadily colder, and I long to have [you] to cuddle up to; you know how jolly well you can do it. I am awfully fit Nell, and I believe I should very nearly squeeze the life right out of you. Oh for the chance to try.

You remember the nail clippers you used to hate so much, kid, they are hopelessly bust. Will you be a pal and get me another pair from Kilpin and Bilsons. If you don't, I shall have to start biting my stumpy nails, and the result will be terrible. I am struggling hard to keep as respectable as possible, so that you will not be too ashamed of me when I come home. Already sweetheart I am getting quite excited at the thought of coming back on leave; you will be glad to see me dearest? Please tell me.

I love you very, very much my darling.

Good-bye my dearest one – my wife.

Yours ever, Frank

Frank, my own darling,

About your three sets of underclothing you ask me to get from Harry
Hills, I hardly know what to do, but I think dear your vests and pants
I have here would be quite alright to send out to you, of course they are
faded, I mean those that you got from Andersons in the first instance,
pale blue, they are quite warm and in fairly good condition so Frank dear
I shall not order the new ones, at least not until I hear from you about
them, so please darling write me at once, because I myself think they
would be quite as well worn out, and I do not think you would find them
too heavy.

I am writing to Hills about your shirts, probably today, there are four
khaki shirts of yours upstairs but I am not sure if they fit you, but the
two Jaeger ones are a filthy colour and the other two made by Jenkinson
and Son, Tunbridge Wells would I think be hardly warm enough for the
winter, but sweetheart when you come home you must really help me to
go through your clothes and throw out those you have finished with.

We have nearly finished the Harness Room. I had quite a bit of fun up
there with Wilkins yesterday – everything was very dirty and heaps of
rubbish but I am rather glad we have got through with it, it is certainly
one thing done towards getting out of this beastly hole.

I feel sure that you said in one of your letters that when you came
home and we were talking things over I should probably tell you that
while you were having a good time out there I was being slowly killed at
home, Yes Frank, I shall tell you that because it is absolutely the truth
as far as I am concerned, I do not mind the days so much because I am
always doing something but from about seven until ten o'clock I feel
I shall go frantic and [it is] only the 3rd week in October. I am so sorry
Frank to grumble, but you will understand that things are bad enough
but now Mrs Bonner is having her teeth taken out by a travelling Dentist
man her bright company is somewhat lessened, thank God she goes to
bed out of sight, but darling is it not strange how some people can bear
any amount of pain without getting miserable – as you know sweetheart
I have had to manage to look cheerful when once or twice I thought the
end of the world had arrived for me.

I did get your letter dear, the one thanking me for sending out your British Warm etc., but it did not arrive until after I had written to you about the coat.

Frank dear I am awfully glad you have paid Reids and do not forget to send along the receipt to me, please Frank, and you say you are sending a cheque off to Harry Hills tonight letter dated Oct 16th, have you done so, tell me.

Thanks dear so much for telling me about your congratulations re. your men, I was awfully pleased, how jolly nice kid, and before I forget in this letter, about your tale a week or two ago 'Some Balls', fine kid I loved it. I could just imagine you telling it to me your dear self just as you used to do on Saturday evenings when you had something quite new for me.

My darling is it possible for you to let me have, or instruct for it to be sent, Bertie's silver cigarette case, he asked for it several times when he was at home and has since written for it and Frank, how about my wrist watch [sic] get a move on, kid, and do not for Heaven's sake forget that I have asked you about three times in my letters re. the watch. Sweetheart, this is a long letter is it not and even now I have not told you that I am still loving you and wanting you very badly but I do kid, you know all about it do you not. I think after careful consideration that if only to come down with you in a 1st from St Pancras would be a jolly sight better than nothing, what say you Frank?
Goodbye my husband, take great care of yourself.

Always your very own, Nell

22 October 1915

Frank, my own darling,

Many many thanks for your letter written on the 19th. I love it kid, I think more especially as you speak about the first night I came to you when you said 'May I', you were a darling that night as you were all the nights before, it was a lovely time was it not kid. I thought it strange when I got your letter this morning because last night when I was turning out all the gas I thought of the nights, the first nights I mean,

when we had used to sit in the Bar after Mrs Bonner had gone to bed.
I am like you Frank, I love to think of all those times. I often sit and think
of everything right from the first Sunday, Leighton Buzzard Horse Show,
where you swear I kissed you first which I am quite sure I did not, or even
so you were so damned agitated that you were fixing your wrist watch
[sic] (which you were kindly lending to me) upside down, but my darling
I believe I have told you before that I had not known you long before I felt
there was just something I cannot fully explain to you sweetheart because
I don't quite know, but once or twice almost when I first knew you just
when I gave you your change when my fingers touched your hand.
Why should I have noticed this, why should there have been just that
something that made me feel even then that I wanted you?

You will have got my letter by now dear, the one asking you about
your underclothing, do not delay in replying Frank dear because there
appears to be a great difficulty and delay in procuring things now.

My sweetheart, in your letter where you are talking of the Piano you
say 'and some room too', thank Heaven for that, Frank, this house in the
Winter without anyone near to love one is too comfortless and now that
expenses have to be cut down to extreme, well you ought to know.

Thank you so much darling, yes, my foot is much better. For days
together I have no pain, I am awfully glad, Frank.

I love you my dearest, and am just living and waiting for the day when
I shall meet you at Folkestone.
With all my love my dearest husband,

Your very own, Nell

Sunday, 24 October 1915

Frank, my own darling,

Is it not a confounded nuisance your enclosed letter came this morning
exactly as it is now, quite open, I am just sending it for you to see, please
return it to me kid. I think it is much too bad of people to forward letters
in this way. I am perfectly willing for all my letters to be opened at some
particular Headquarters if necessary, but I do object to say probably the

Ashbys, and the Postman, not forgetting Rose and Mrs Bonner prying into them, but anyway there the thing remains if either of them did read it much good may it do them. I have only to keep very very quiet and I shall soon find out if it was read.

My darling I am so sorry you are going to be moved, I too hope it is not to Servia [sic] but you say although rumour seems to point that way, and you never say these sort of things unless you are nearly sure. I shall be frightfully anxious, Frank, but I suppose I must hope for the best.

I think this War is too terrible sweetheart and in places like this very depressing because one has to go on from weekend to weekend listening to uneducated people's opinions which gives me the creeps. I often and always wish you were here Frank to talk to me and explain to me about the War but that is not the only thing I want you to be back for. I want you to be back with me for always and always but as I have said in my letter, I suppose I must hope for the best, but I get so jolly tired of hoping and waiting. Your letter has made me rather miserable kid, I hate the idea of your going away from France, and darling please tell me, have you made arrangements in case of anything happening to you that I am told at once, you did tell me before you went away that you would arrange all this but I am afraid you may have forgotten, tell me Frank, please. But nothing is going to happen to you, not really, you are going to come back to me and one day we are going to be married.

I do not think you were very happy when you wrote the enclosed to me, what was the matter Frank dear?

It is a beastly day here today, raining the whole of the time and a bitterly cold wind but up to yesterday kid we have had topping weather and many days through this month up to now we have not had fires.

I am so glad darling you are awfully well, that is a great comfort to me. Cheer up my own darling and write to me, please tell me all about the envelope being opened, why do they do this Frank? It might have been jolly awkward if Bertie had been at home.
All my love sweetheart,

Your very own, Nell

27 October 1915

My own sweetheart,

I am sending you some cigarettes and tobacco. You poor darling, of course I will send you some each week, I did not know or at least I was not quite clear that you wished me to do so and please, Frank, tell me the exact quantity you would like sent out, I mean dear each week, and do you like the Richmond Gem cigarettes or would you rather I sent some other sort?

Yesterday I was inclined to send off to you your vests and pants, the old ones, but after getting your letter this morning I am jolly glad I did not do so although I have repaired them very beautifully but once or twice, Frank, when I was working on them I did wonder if they had shrunk, they appeared to me small. Yes, I quite agree with you darling where you say your extensive back parts, do you remember how many times we have laughed about it and I have made you bend down in the bathroom, of course you have always told me that mine is nothing to write home about, but personally I am quite satisfied, but sweetheart I will send off to Hills today about your underclothes and see what I can do, and will forward them to you as soon as possible.

Your letter this morning is very much brighter than the last two received from you. I am awfully glad and quite excited about the saxe blue tabs on your shoulder straps, why is this darling? Please tell me all about it, yes, I do love the colour (saxe blue) and when I am really well off I shall buy some very lovely clothes in this particular colour.

I have been expecting your Chelsea Bank notepaper but up to the present it has not arrived so it must come along with your vests and pants because I dare not wait any longer in sending off your cigarettes and tobacco. I am frightened now about the delay.

I hope you will like the Nail Clippers I am sending to you. I could not get them quite like your old ones, candidly I do not quite remember the design but I think these quite nice.

About the tunic buttons dear you asked about, you have only the one tunic here, at least with the East Lancashire buttons, three tunics altogether, so what have I to do sweetheart, have I to cut off the buttons and send them to you? I think it will be rather a pity to do so because when you are home will you not be able to wear this particular tunic?

Shall I order you some buttons from Reids, if so how many? Frank dear please tell me, have you paid their bill? And do not forget to write me about the buttons.

Yes, I suppose the Dentistry will be paid from the Separation Allowance, also the new Grey Furs, etc. etc. You say what happens when Fletcher comes down for the weekend, I do not know but damned little I should imagine, when he is home she waits until quite late Saturday evening and then she says 'Do you mind if I sleep out tonight?' Frank, I am frightfully amused. When she asks me this and I dare not look at her I just say no, certainly not, so then we have supper, I go to bed and she goes out after and she returns in time to cook the breakfast Sunday morning. I think even now she has a letter from him every day, as I said in my letter darling it has not been mentioned between us. I am glad I could not talk about it because I think the thing is absolutely wrong.

My own dearest I am glad you are getting on so well with your job and giving every satisfaction, please keep on going kid, I am awfully proud of you and love you so much.

I will write again very soon darling. Goodbye my husband, with all my love.

Your very own, Nell
P.S. You must read this letter very carefully Frank because there is [sic] several things you have to reply to and please may I have Reids, also Harry Hills receits [sic].

                                                    29 October 1915

Frank, dearest,
I do not feel very much like writing today, but I want to write just a short letter to you my darling. I received your little letter dated October 26th where you had just received orders to move in a hurry, I am so sorry Frank you are leaving France, somehow, kid, I do not know why but I feel particularly depressed about it. I have the idea of you going still further away from me.

I wonder if the tobacco and cigarettes etc. that I posted to you from here Wednesday last, 27th, have reached you, I hope they have kid.

I received the enclosed from Harry Hills this morning, thanks Frank dear, I will take care of the receipt for you kid and I am awfully glad it is paid. You are a darling, you do try to please me sometimes, do you not?

You said in one of your letters let me know how you are getting on with your packing up, not at all Frank, I am cross about it really because you see, kid, there is so little I can pack until quite the last and then there would be quite a lot of stuff – of course as I told you before the Harness Room is quite finished, there is nothing left at all there with the exception of the one large box. I have done quite a lot of turning out indoors and I have one case packed with china. The whole thing is so very uncertain one does not know how long this dreadful war is going to last, but immediately there is the tiniest of whispers about the end I shall then make <u>some move</u>. When I send your underclothes (I am expecting them tomorrow) I am sending you a topping print – you must pin it up somewhere and of course darling if you move on again you must leave it behind.

I shall be awfully anxious for your next letter, please tell me sweetheart as much as you can about the place you are in also about the War, the Daily Papers for over a week have not been by any means bright, and more especially tell me about your own dear self. I love you Frank my husband, my own darling, goodbye, soon dear I will write to you again.

Your wife, Nell

30 October 1915

Frank, my own darling,

I got the enclosed letter from Harry Hills this morning and Frank dear I hardly know what to do about it, but I am writing to him today asking him to procure at his earliest the vests with the ½ sleeves, I do not think you would like the long sleeves unless dear you would prefer them for the extra warmth, but please write me by return saying if you would like the long sleeved vests because if Hills is a long time in procuring the ½ sleeves I may have got your reply in the meantime and if you think you would like them I might be able to send the others on first or will you wait for the short sleeves? I am quite sure he ought to get them quickly, surely men 20 years of age in England do not cuddle themselves up in long sleeved vests.

I had a most unsatisfactory post this morning, numbers of bills, and a letter from Bertie saying he is having a fortnight's leave in November, he is already complaining rather bitterly about his expenses etc. but that part of the business he can get on with, he did not go into it with his eyes shut.

I have just remembered you asked for some Nutta boot polish, I have been to Fox's and he has only got it in the light shade, so he is procuring two tins for you as before, but I have just discovered a nearly full tin of yours upstairs so when I send your tobacco next week I will enclose it. The 30th of October today and sweetheart it is a topping day here, the sun beautifully warm. I should imagine it would be delightful motoring today.

I am frightfully sorry, Frank, about the delay in your underclothes but it makes it rather awkward kid in having to procure everything through the post – if I had been going out I could in all probability have procured them elsewhere but you will not mind will you Frank, not very much, and I am so afraid you may think I have not bothered about them but I have, kid, and I hate the delay.

I did not have a letter from you yesterday or today, of course I shall miss your letters very much but I shall not mind, because I know sweetheart you will post to me at your earliest opportunity. I love you Frank dear and soon, very soon may you come safely home to me, I want you to come home so badly. My darling all my love is yours, but you know, I have told you so often, and you are glad are you not?
Goodbye my husband,
Your own, Nell

Wednesday, 30 October 1915

Frank, my own darling,

Many thanks for your letter received this morning, the one written on the 9th. Frank dear I cannot quite understand when you say you had not had a letter from me for a week. I feel more than convinced now that you do not get all the letters that I write to you because I have written to you practically every other day and sometimes every day with about three exceptions and quite the longest time was three days in between, you say a week kid. I am jolly glad I have not had to wait a week before hearing from you, I should be frightfully anxious, but you have been very good to me in writing quite often, thank you darling so much.

I had a letter from you Monday, and yesterday being Tuesday I did not hear from you. I was awfully disappointed, I said to Mrs Bonner no letter for me? She said yes, there are two, I said yes I know, but I mean not one from Captain Smith – if you had seen her expression you would have been amused.

I am glad you are going to tell me about what you think I ought to do with the house. I am anxious to hear your suggestions and understand, sweetheart, this time no evading things, I am perfectly willing to try to manage the Winter for say another six months but of course I shall get further and further into debt. Frank dear I wonder if I really ought to get rid of Mrs Bonner, of course she is married although it has not been mentioned between us, but I feel there is so little for them both to do and nothing doing in the way of trade. I should not mind explaining things to Mrs Bonner now she is provided for, or would you suggest that Rose should go, that is of course if Mrs Bonner is willing to undertake the work, tell me Frank dear please. I am sorry in a way to bother you about these sort of things because I know you have heaps of work and worry out there, but even when you were at home I have surprised myself in the way I had used to ask you for your advice. I never remember asking any other man about the different little things that I always feel I must ask you about, why is it Frank? It can only be because I love you so much. I do love you, you say in your letter 'write and tell me you know I want you', yes dear, I do know you want me and I am glad, and I believe you want me in the same way as I want you, just that particular longing, Frank, where nobody else in the whole world will do.

I have sometimes wondered (but I always try to put these thoughts away, they frighten me) what I should do if anything happens to you out there and you do not live to come home, I should be heartbroken and all interest in life for me would be gone, of course I should still have the kid

but even she would not be able to help me, but please God nothing will
happen to you and you will come back to me, and then, my husband,
I will prove to you that you are everything to me – want you, my darling,
yes, in all ways.
Please write to me.

Your wife, Nell
P.S. I am puzzled, kid, tell me, in your letter where you said and if you try
to be rude for Heaven's sake spell correctly, was the word 'believe'?

2 November 1915

Frank, my own darling,

I have not had a letter from you for four whole days, today is Tuesday
and I have not heard from you since last Thursday and in consequence
the intervening days have seemed years but I know it is not your fault my
sweetheart, you did explain to me that I was not to mind if I did not hear
from you for a few days so I am still keeping on hoping for the best.
    I am sending your tobacco and cigarettes, also matches. I do not know
if you want them, I mean the matches, also your Nutta polish, notepaper,
and if I receive the envelopes by this afternoon post I will enclose a few,
the envelopes darling that came in the first instance were very large so
I returned them asking for them to be exchanged for a smaller size, and
I understand by a note received this morning that they are in the post.
I thought sweetheart as most of the paper and envelopes would be used
for me, I should prefer the small size as I usually carry one or two of your
letters about with me, I love your letters kid, please tell me Frank dear
most of it will be used for me will it not?
    I have no news darling as everything goes on in the same old way.
A number of the Toddington men that are with the Expeditionary Force
have been home for their week's holiday. I understand that Whinnett
and the man Smith, you know dear, the man that married Whinnett's
sister, and took the farm at Tebworth, have had a terrific row. They had a
Benning over from Dunstable and Cumberland from Luton to straighten
things out for them. I am jolly glad, personally I should think that Smith

wishes old man Whinnett had lived somewhat longer so that he could have finished his deal with Messrs Norbury Smith & Co.

The enclosed post card came this morning. I am glad dear, I hope they will be satisfactory, if so I will send them to you immediately, and next week I ought to be able to send you shirts.

Frank darling are you still keeping on loving me? I hope you are, I slept awfully badly last night and the whole of the time I was awake I was thinking about you, I wonder, kid, what our own bedroom will be really like, it must be a large room Frank.

I did not finish this letter this morning. The envelopes have not arrived so they must come along with your vests etc. but I have got your tiny letter dated Oct 29th where you say you may not be able to get another letter off for seven days. I shall understand darling, thank you so much my husband for the tiny letter, yes, I will keep on writing to you and you say please keep on loving me a wee bit so, Frank, not a wee bit but with all the love I am capable of, for now and always my own sweetheart. Goodbye my darling.

Your wife, Nell

5 November 1915

Frank, my darling,

I miss your letters so much; I had no real idea I should miss them quite as I do and I am dreadfully afraid that something may happen to you now that they have sent you away from France. I shall perhaps feel better about things, Frank, when I hear from you again often. This place is frightfully depressing and of course will be all through the Winter but I should feel just the same about you Frank dear wherever I was living, nothing could allay my anxious thoughts about you, you see I love you so much which makes all the difference in the world does it not? And all I can do is to remain quietly at home and hope and pray you will come safely back to me.

I am awfully glad I am able to send some of your warm shirts and part of your underclothing today, of course sweetheart I have them all here but the box will not hold any more so I will send the remainder next week. I do not mind now, you have some to go on with. I wonder if you will like them, please tell me when next you write. I think you will find them beautifully warm.

You have once or twice remarked about my warm comfy nighties, I do not know how you can speak about them, not really, because I am quite sure you have never been near me when I have been wearing one but what I was going to say darling is that your shirts are made from material like my nighties, only, sweetheart, in a different shade.

Frank, tell me just at the present moment would you like to be near me, or rather to sleep with me just for one night. I am frightfully tired of sleeping by myself, just fed up, I hate it, then again I suppose there is no real necessity for me to do this only there is nobody else, only you, but kid I just want to be near you awfully badly. Frank, honestly, if only just to touch you, stroke your hair, just any tiny little thing if it was only you would comfort me more than I could ever explain on paper [sic]. I just want you and I feel as if I have every right to you, you gave yourself to me absolutely a long time ago, did you not again tell me, and 'I', well you know, sometimes when I think of my indifference to Bertie, my home, and everything I had used to be interested in I feel almost like crying and sometimes, not very often, I wonder if I am sailing too near the wind. I suppose if Bertie really found out now and if he questioned me anyways closely I should admit to everything, I am sure I should, and then, Frank, if you did not come back well even then I should have to take my chance, but that would not worry me for long because without my husband I should not want to live, neither should I. Tell me, you would loose [sic] a lot of interest in life would you not Frank? if I was suddenly taken away from you, and you love me as you have never loved any other woman. I want so badly to be told just today and when you have read this please write to me one of your nice letters and as you have said in your letters please please keep on loving me.
I worship you. Goodbye dearest,

Your wife, Nell

8 November 1915

Frank, my own darling,

I am just going to write to you a tiny letter to tell you I am still waiting patiently for a letter from you, a week today since I last heard, seven days ago kid, and the days have seemed so long. I could not go on, Frank dear, without your letters, and the last three days I have felt frightfully unsettled, felt that I really must go out somewhere, and you would not like it if I did go out. I feel sure you would not, at least not in the mood I was in then, but I did not go. Would you mind awfully kid if I did go out some evening, of course you would, I suppose I must judge your feelings in this kind of thing with my own. Frank dear, if you only took out to dinner one of your own sisters, I believe I should be so frightfully jealous that I should be almost mad.

If ever you do give me cause to be jealous my darling, I should be just one of the unhappiest women alive, but I don't think you would Frank, would you? You love me by far too much, I know you love me and just once or twice when I have felt that I would go out I have gone upstairs and just got your photograph – I mean the one head and shoulders where I can see so plainly your eyes – I have then thought of all the lovely times we have had together, and all the glorious times we are going to have, and then I feel better and I just think not for anything in the world would I go out, or do the tiniest thing that would cause him a moment's anxiety and more so now my darling, now that you are right out there.

Goodbye Frank my husband, I love you, please please write to me.

Always your very own, Nell

11 November 1915

Frank, my own darling,

It is two whole days since I last wrote to you and up to now sweetheart no letter from you. I wonder if you will get all the letters I am sending to you, there are three parcels to be acknowledged, Frank I have sent you two parcels with tobacco etc. and then part of your shirts, vests and pants, etc.

I have not been feeling a tiny bit well just lately but I suppose it
is because I am worrying a little bit, ever such a tiny bit, about you
and then today is quite the wrong time of the month for me and I feel
wretched and depressed as I believe I have said in one or two of my letters.
I shall feel better when I hear from you.

How are you Frank dear, are you quite well and fairly happy? I hope
you are. My darling you have no real idea as to what Toddington is like
now, night after night we have no one in, not even one single person,
and even out of doors no lights visible, is it not too ridiculous? The lights
from the houses have had to be to a certain extent darkened, but that
makes not the slightest difference to me because I never go out after dark
with the exception to the letter box and even that I cannot find without
groping for it.

Are you still loving me sweetheart, please tell me, I am always thinking
about you, my own darling, always loving you. During the last week
I have cried several times, I am afraid for you, kid, and I want so badly
for you to be back with me, I do not mean just for your leave I mean for
always my husband, of course dear your leave when it comes will be
lovely, I often think about it and Frank please promise me on your oath
kid that you will not leave me in London as you did before, my God
Frank if you do I will make you sorry for it. Even now I sometimes feel
that I have to get my own back over that but we shall see.

I have paid Fleckney, I owed him quite a lot of money but £2.15.6 of the
account is yours, you will very shortly have to send me another allowance
now, £1.0.0. per week is some money when one is badly off, but I am really
quite cheerful. Frank, you have promised to see me through and I know
you love me which means such a lot to me when I am weary and troubled.
Goodbye my own darling,

Your wife-to-be, Nell

15 November 1915

Frank, my own darling,

A fortnight ago today, kid, I had a tiny letter from you in which you said please keep on writing dearest – Frank I just feel as if I cannot write to you again until I hear from you. I keep on waiting and waiting for your letter, 14 days, kid, but there now you must know exactly how I feel about everything and of course dear I do not blame you, but at times I think it is all very well being stuck away down here, it is a real good job I did not know what things were going to be like, if I had known I am quite sure I would not have promised to be absolutely good.

Are you still loving me Frank? I asked you this in my last letter about three days ago, tell me you have never loved anyone else since you have known me, have you kid and during the time you have been away from me, 3 months, 12 long weeks I suppose darling really I ought to be ashamed of myself in asking you this but you did once tell me not only once but several times that it was rubbish for me to tell you that I was sure Tommy never went astray, but Frank you must tell me in your next letter that you are still living absolutely for me and please please be kind to me, don't be cross Frank dear.

I cannot help it kid, I am jolly miserable and the delay of not hearing from you worries me frightfully.

My darling I love you so much but I need not tell you this over and over again in my letters, you know exactly how much I love you, nobody can know better than you Frank just what your coming into my life has meant to me. You know darling what beastly moods I get into and sometimes I almost convince myself you will change your mind about marrying me, is it not too stupid sweetheart? How could you live without me or ever want to do so after all we have been to each other, husband and wife have we not? in the very truest sense of the word. My God Frank if anything should happen to you out there and I should never see you again I should be left with not the tiniest interest in the world, would it not be very dreadful? I wonder sometimes if I love you too much, but no it is not possible, please write to me.

Always darling,

Your very own, Nell

TELEGRAM
Armstrong
Toddington
Dunstable
England

All well. Many thanks love.

Frank

17 November 1915

Frank, my own darling,

I have started this letter because I just feel I must write to you but honestly kid I do not feel very much like writing. I have just been wondering if Miss Acheson was married before you left England darling because I think, Frank, she married the man Martin you once spoke of, her husband is a Lieut by the name of Martin from Woburn Sands way, she has been married a few months, but since I started this letter I have pieced the thing together, if it is the same man it would be more than strange would it not because during the time he was with you he must have been thinking of marrying this girl from the Wain Holm, but at the same time unless he is frightfully religious I think I feel rather sorry for him but perhaps if she has a large family (I hope so), it may improve her.

I did get one of Vickery's Khaki Bronze frames for your photograph, not one of the heavy ones – I did not like the No. X3010, at least dear not for the head and shoulders photograph, so I returned it and asked them to send the No. X3011 at £1.17.6, no I mean £1.13.6 which is most suitable and quite nice, most of the time darling it stands on the shelf in my bedroom and I look at it many many times through the day and I do occasionally bring it down onto the table here where I am writing and often, Frank dear, immediately I am out of bed in the mornings I just stand and gaze at it and even this morning with the snow all round about after Mrs Bonner had brought up my tea I just hopped out of bed and started my lamp going and then back into bed for a long minute just for the room to get warm, but I took your dear photograph back into bed with me and had a real good look at it. I love it sweetheart, although at times when I want you so badly it is poor comfort. I had a letter this morning from Mrs Rawkins, she is rather keen on me going with her to a dance that is coming off at Dunstable, something to do with the Engineers at Houghton Regis.

How strange Frank, I had just got this far in my letter when someone came in and it was Ethel, and just as she arrived a letter from Bertie saying he will be home today week for a day or two. I was awfully pleased to see Ethel, but damned annoyed about Bertie coming home. I have not decided about the dance but I really think, Frank, as he is coming home then I shall go, it will be one night away from the house during the time he is here, and you will not mind my darling because you know I love you far too much ever to trouble the tiniest bit about anyone else.

Seventeen days dearest and no letter. I think when it does arrive and should it come on the first post I shall not get up at all that day because it will be some letter, it must be. I am not very happy when I think of having no letters from you. I just sit and eat my finger nails [sic] sometimes when I am very anxious about you. My husband I love you, my own true darling are you not?

Please write to me,

Your wife, Nell

22 November 1915

Frank, my own darling,

I am feeling a little bit better, only a little bit, today but Frank dear if I could just have sat down Saturday night and wrote to you I should have asked you to give me up, and as I was feeling then I should have meant it, kid, but let me explain, Bertie is home for a fortnight's leave – he got here Saturday morning in time for breakfast. Of course the day wore on in its usual style, Randall brought from Luton a most lovely box of chocolates, Bertie must have ordered them in the morning. During the evening I could have had heaps and heaps to drink, which I very firmly refused, and then when he found immediately after 10 o'clock that he was not to sleep in my room he refused supper and after Mrs Bonner had gone to bed a most dreadful scene; I cannot explain, on paper it could not be described, but you Frank, if you love me as much as I love you, should know exactly how I felt. I am ill today, quite ill really, why does he keep on coming back here, Frank, as I told him before and as I told him again on Saturday night to end the whole thing. I don't care what he does, I only know that after he has been home I am very poorly. I worry the whole of the time he is here and sleep is out of the question, all I do is just lie in bed and stare out into the night. If only you were awfully well off Frank so that I could be absolutely independent of him and the home, it would make things so much easier for me. I suppose in a way I am a fool; it is a poor woman that cannot manage two men but there the thing remains. I love you as I have never loved anyone else and the result is that no other man can even touch me, not whilst I feel about you as I feel now, but don't you yourself wish you could take me right away from him now so that I need not be so worried and troubled?

I think it is about three days since I wrote to you, but I have had your letter, kid, the one written on the S.S. Ezra and posted I think at Malta. I was awfully glad to get it sweetheart and I am much looking forward to your next long letter, the sort of Diary you speak of that you are writing up for me.

Bertie is just coming in, he has been over to Hockliffe so darling I cannot write any more. Please please trust me sweetheart, as far as I am concerned he came here so he will go away and you know this, but there is one thing that you will never quite know and that is just how the whole thing affects me, I sometimes and often think I am a woman apart, just somebody not quite like other women. I wonder if I am, if so why was I born like this? Because at times I am damned unhappy.
Goodbye my husband-to-be,

Your very own, Nell
P.S. Frank my darling, I will write to you again the very first opportunity, but now it is difficult.

24 November 1915

Frank, my own darling,

I have got your new address so I am sending the remainder of your underclothes and shirts. Frank you must forgive these letters if they are not quite so bright as they might be, the truth is kid I am worried almost to death, by now you will have got my letter telling you that Bertie is home for a fortnight, even now there is only three days of the time gone. God knows what I shall be like at the end of the fortnight, several more lines and wrinkles I suppose, and my hair with luck perhaps only grey, but it may be white.

You are a darling, this morning I had two letters from you, the registered one dated Nov 10th and the next one dated the 11th. Sweetheart thank you so much for the £20 cheque, you are indeed good to me, during the last day or two I had felt a tiny bit troubled about Bob's Christmas account but now I shall feel better about that again, thank you very much.

You say in both your letters please please love me now, I need it more than ever. I do love you, worship you Frank, I am sure I do, and during the last few days I have thought about you and wondered about everything more than ever. I do not know if Bertie really does get more foolish or perhaps I am growing old, but his damned emptyheadedness (good word that) astonishes me. The other night after 10 o'clock of course he was still on about the same old thing when he said, do you mean to tell me that after the War and I do manage to get some money together, and something to do that you will not then live with me as my wife? I said I did not know, I had not made up my mind, and ever since then nothing more has been said about it. I hope to God this time when he gets back he will write to Durance and settle the whole thing. I do not want him, neither do I want his money, I can work until it is convenient for me to come to you my darling, but there now I shall bother you if I keep on Frank, so now how about your cigarettes? I think I have asked you before to tell me if the kind I am sending you is what you like.

I have no real news. Bobby was delighted with your letter, thank you so much Frank dear for writing to her.

I have send [sic] you quite a number of letters, also three parcels apart from this one. I do hope you get them, I am anxious to hear. You have acknowledged my letter dated Oct 24th, I think that was the one handed to you at Marseilles, and then in one of your letters this morning you speak of my letter dated Oct 30th but I wrote to you Oct 27th enclosed with tobacco etc., also a letter again on 29th, but perhaps by now you have received them.

Goodbye my husband, Frank dear, I want you and love you always.

Your wife-to-be, Nell

26 November 1915

Frank dearest,

I posted you a parcel yesterday – the 25th – the remainder of your shirts and underclothes, I also sent you some tobacco dear, and cigarettes, 'Some parcel' I assure you I am afraid I used terrific language about it, of course dear I was anxious as soon as I received your new address to send off the remaining things etc. so packed the parcel in the usual way with brown paper and string, I had a frightful job really in getting it off at all with him about, because writing to you now is almost like stealing something, and then when I got it into the Post Office Miss Ashby expressed great regret in not being able to accept it owing to it not being stitched in a linen cover, name etc. not being written on in ink etc. etc. but is it not .....'s, you know, Frank, a word that is spelt with five letters, I felt jolly well inclined to tell her so. But kid dear, tell me about the parcel when it reaches you, I guess you will be amused.

Miss Ashby said she thought the parcels would be a lot of trouble to the people that were sending them out to the Mediterranean Force, but she forgets or probably has never known that there are parcels and parcels.

Your parcels, my darling, would never be any trouble to me Frank, I would sit up all the night through to send you just whatever you wanted, I have told you this I feel sure in many of my letters, and please darling never be afraid to ask me for anything you want sent out.

Poor old Joan is staying here, the Rent Dinner is Wednesday next, Dec 1st. I wonder if this will be the last dinner I shall be here for, or if I shall be here for the one in June. I keep on wondering and thinking kid darling, but it does not seem to do very much good, but we shall be able to talk things over when you are home for your leave more definitely kid this time than we have ever been able to before. I love you awfully and I feel in nearly everything I should like to take your advice but Frank there is nothing, absolutely nothing on God's earth that would persuade me to stay on in this house through the Winter of 1916, War or no War I do not care a damn, so tell me please when you write that we will talk things over when you are home and that you will try to arrange for me.

During the last few days I have frightful nerves and neuralgia but one can hardly expect anything else. I often think Frank dear about our first Winter after we are married. I mean sweetheart I wonder what it will be really like, I know it will be just lovely, tell me darling, can you describe it?

Last evening once or twice it struck me very forcibly, particularly so when I was crawling up and down the cellar steps, frightfully cold, very unhappy and just waiting for bed time.

A more than perfect time we will have together, I will be awfully good to you my dear one and you will be kind to me and love me always Frank dear please, I know you will. If my darling, after we are married, I noticed the tiniest sign of you tiring of me I should be heartbroken. God forbid this should ever happen.

Take great care of yourself and please tell me in your next letter if you are keeping well, I hope so kid.
All my love my darling,

Your very own, Nell

29 November 1915

Frank, my own darling,

Thirteen weeks yesterday since I last saw you and I have loved you every minute since then, loved you absolutely my husband not in a half hearted sort of way, but with every tiny bit of love my whole being is capable of. Frank dear, Mrs Bonner is awfully amused because nearly every Sunday night I just say Thank God one more Sunday gone, she thinks it is very dreadful to wish the time gone, but I tell her I wish all the weeks gone like flashes of lightning until you come back, she laughs, kid, and says she can hardly believe it – I do not wonder, I have been no greater surprise to anyone than to myself.

I do not think I am going to get letters from you very often. I had your two letters Wednesday last and I have not heard since, but even so I shall not mind sweetheart because in your letter you said I will manage to get letters through to you as regularly as it is humanly possible, thank you so much, I know you will, you are a dear kid, I am loving you awfully just now and I wish real hard you were here in more ways than one, because you know Frank dear what always happens when I do love you just a baby bit more than usual, you remember do you not my darling? I sent you a letter dated Nov 15th, have you got it? In this letter I asked you quite a lot and I still want you to tell me that right from the time you have known me no other woman has had a second thought where you are concerned. If you say no other woman ever has, some people would say rubbish I do not believe him. I do not mind what other people would say or think because they do not understand the amount of real love there is between us. I am sure, kid, our love is a very different kind of love to what comes to a very great majority of people. I love you, and it is because I know that you love me in the same way that I am happy.

Only two more whole days and Bertie will be gone, I shall be jolly pleased. I have been thinking, Frank, if later on when things have to be explained to him very plainly I do not think he will die of a broken heart. I have found out one or two little things since he has been home this time. He has been frightfully careful about his letters but two I have managed to read, one from a woman in Canada who signs herself 'Your own kid', the second letter from a woman at the Curragh, 'Some letter' this second one, I assure you she speaks of him as a great big beautiful man, and goes on to say that she wants him to come back so that she can creep right into his arms. I do not think if I had sufficient money I should find a great difficulty in obtaining my divorce. The astonishing part of the whole thing to me is, that in [the] face of this he expects to come to me here etc., etc. and then when he finds he is not to come to my room he gets into a rage, but I quite believe it is a case of wounded vanity and that if I am no good to him from that point of view he has no further use for me, 'Thank God'.

My darling this is quite a long letter but he is up in Town today
so I have not been disturbed so many times over it, but I must finish
now dear and I will perhaps write to you again tomorrow. All my love
my husband-to-be, take great care of yourself and please write to me.
Goodbye dear,

You very own, Nell

3 December 1915

Frank, my own darling,

No kid, I do not think I am getting all your letters because I have received
a letter from you dated Nov 11th and then the next letter I got was dated
Nov 18th, a week, Frank, in between and then dear this morning I got
two letters from you, the registered one with the coins dated Nov 22nd
and the second one dated Nov 23rd. I am sorry my darling you have
not been getting my letters. Yes Frank, I have written to you quite a lot,
nearly every other day and sometimes every day, but this week I have not
been able to write to you quite so much. I posted to you on Monday last,
29th, and not again until today, Friday, forgive me please sweetheart but
I could not help it. Tuesday last some officer men came here and asked if
they could use the house as Headquarters, they had a very large scheme
on, they came from Baldock, that is near Biggleswade you know, they
were here from 10 o'clock Tuesday morning until 10 o'clock Wednesday
morning working the whole night through. Officers and men were
sleeping all over the house. I got to bed at about 3.30 a.m. on Wednesday
morning and then of course the Rent Dinner on this day, the Farmers
stayed until 10 o'clock, or rather most of them, all of them very merry
and bright, 'Attwood very drunk', you see it was Bertie's last night, he
returned to the Curragh yesterday, Thursday, the fact of it being his
last night made them drink more stuff than usual, so I am sure you will
understand when I say that Wednesday night I went to bed a very tired
and sorry woman, bored absolutely stiff.

The officer men were quite a cheery crowd and I think in a way quite
enjoyed themselves. The Colonel was a dear man. In a way I was glad

they came because it made it so damned awkward for Bertie, of course
through the day he had to clear off somewhere and in the evening he
and old Murray sat in Murray's bedroom and drank much whisky and
soda, which dear Ivan had to fetch from the bar as Rose was rushed
in the other part of the house, of course they had a nice fire and were
jolly comfy up there. I felt too knocked up to write to you yesterday
sweetheart but I am quite alright today. Now about your dear self, poor
old Frank, I am so very sorry, you are indeed having a rough time. Are
you really getting thin? I do hope by now you have got your thick shirts
and underclothes, I posted the first lot to you Nov 5th so by now Frank
they should have reached you. How dreadful it must be to be so cold. My
darling in your reply to this letter tell me if there is anything else I can
send you, do not be the tiniest bit afraid to ask me. I say do not be the
tiniest bit afraid, how stupid of me – of course you would not be afraid to
ask. I am your woman am I not? And you are my one man in the whole
world, I love you.

In one of your letters this morning you say Thank heaven this month
is nearly over and you will soon be alone again, nothing has happened
I hope dearest. No my darling, he has gone away once more. He came
home on Saturday Nov 20th and returned yesterday, Thursday Dec 2nd,
13 days and <u>nothing has happened.</u> I think only once did he come into my
bedroom and then I was fully dressed, but you will have got my other
letters by now or at least some of them and in them I have explained
to you quite a lot and when you come home Frank we are going to talk
things over very seriously this time, are we not? Tell me.

Your letter I got yesterday and the two this morning have done me
quite a lot of good, thank you so much kid, please please keep on loving me
and pray God to send you safely back to me. I often cry about you Frank
and now you are right away from me (not in France, things never seemed
quite so bad when you were there) I am truly afraid. I do not think I am
quite so afraid you will get killed as I used to be but one thing I am afraid
of and that is that you may get very ill and nobody [will be] there to
nurse you.

Frank darling, when do you think you will try to get home? Tell me in
your next letter, I wonder when, sweetheart mine, I love you very dearly.
Take great care of yourself for my sake, for the woman's sake, Frank, who

loves you more than anything on earth and who feels that without you
she cannot live.

My husband, goodbye until tomorrow when I will write you again.
Always my darling.

Your very own, Nell

4 December 1915

My own darling boy,

I do not know how many times I have read your two letters that I got
yesterday but many times sweetheart. I love them, thank you so much.
Ivan left here this morning, thank God he has gone, he has been here
since last Wednesday week. I thought it was rather strange this morning
when he said goodbye to me, he said would I be here for the next dinner
in June, I told him I was not at all sure about anything, but if I left in
the meantime I would write to him. I have not mentioned a tiny word to
him about leaving, but no doubt Bertie has said something to him, if not,
then dear Joan has very carefully weighed up my damned indifference
to everything.

Frank darling in my last two letters I quite forgot to tell you that Mrs
Bonner is leaving me. I think she is supposed to be going on the 24th of
this month but no doubt she will stay over Christmas now. Frank dear
you are not to worry and wonder if I shall be alright without her because
of course I shall. I do not mind a tiny bit, not really, she is so very quiet
and miserable, but what made her decide to leave me was 1st Sonny
Bonner has been living with the Ayres and a week or two ago they asked
for more money per week. 2nd I think she found it anything but nice when
the polished Horace came home for the weekends in having to stay with
his people. She has taken a tiny cottage and darling the day she told me
she was leaving me she cried and said how sorry she was. In a way I was
sorry for her and at the same time astonished.

Heavens, Frank, I wonder if I thought of leaving here to prepare a
home where I was going to live with you, if I should cry. No, a thousand
times no. I should be almost mad with excitement, everything about the

place here could go to blazes. I do not quite know how I shall manage without her but I shall try very hard because for the short time I shall be here I do not want to engage anyone else and Mrs Bonner says she will be able to come in when I want her, of course that arrangement would be all very well but it would not be quite like having someone in the house altogether, but we shall see dear.

There is one thing very certain about it and that is her being away from the house will not make the slightest bit of difference to me when you are coming home on leave because if I have only poor Rose to leave in charge I shall come to meet you, and apart from coming to meet you I shall not return here for at least two nights and during that time I shall not lose sight of you, not even for you to go out to buy, let me think, what was it, Safety Razors or French Letters to take away to France with you, I forget which, then there was that business of having your boots and leggings cleaned, all I believe on the same day, Aug 28th 1915. Of course, I have not forgotten the time when I lost you altogether in London for about two whole days but I think really you had some other woman then, tell me, did you?

I love you Frank my husband, do you love me? I wish you were here just this very moment to hold me for five minutes, to hold me as tight and as close to you as possible, and then, well you know, would you like it kid darling? Do you think it would do you quite a lot of good? I should love it, just you my darling. Please tell me about your leave, it will soon be four long months since I last saw you and I am starving for you Frank. I want to be near you so badly sometimes, I could not explain.
Goodbye my true darling, are you not?
Please write to me.

Your wife, Nell

                                                        7 December 1915

Frank, my own darling,

I received another letter from you Sunday morning the one dated Nov 15th although some days before this I got your letter dated Nov 23rd so the 15th one took 20 days to get here. I am awfully glad it has arrived because, Frank dear, it is the one containing the diary of your journey right to the time of your leaving Alexandria, thank you so much kid, it is awfully interesting and do not forget to let me have the remainder. I was awfully amused in several parts of it and, Frank, where you say about the three men 'notorious characters' 2 Francs worth each. Great game this, and where you say you decide to turn a blind eye to this rather natural indiscretion. You dear darling, how jolly nice you stick things down on paper, but are you not always the same, it was that topping way of yours that when I first knew you appealed to me frightfully, and then my darling the first night I came down to your room when you said 'May I?', just again that jolly nice way of yours I loved you Frank and right from then as far as I was concerned the whole thing was settled, you crept into my life I am sure right from that particular moment, ever since then I have lived absolutely for you. I have never had a second thought for anyone else and it will always be the same Frank my husband, even supposing things do not turn out as I trust and pray they will, even supposing that after all we do not get married I should always love you, you would be to me the one man I had really and truly loved, and sometimes when I was alone I should cry a tiny bit about everything, but I should always want you to be happy. My God Frank how I love you. I wonder if you really know how much.

How strange one of your people speaking of the man who always drank Champagne for breakfast, Frank Otter. Poor old Frank, I wonder where he is? I have not seen him for ages. Pickering from Hockliffe was in the other day and was rather chipping me about the day when I went to Uckfield to say goodbye to Bertie, then he went on to say how did I manage it to say goodbye to Bertie and then the other chap to motor me from Town on the same day. Quite the wrong end of the tale he had got hold of because if you remember we came by train to Harlington, but I thought it was pretty plain proof that someone had been gossipy, but even so, kid, it is not very surprising, I think perhaps we have given them many opportunities, what say you darling?

I was rather surprised really when Pickering mentioned this because it is such a long time ago, last May, but things like this make me hate and detest the particular class of people that come here more than usual, but

apart from all the gossip I shall be jolly glad when we are married. I feel a
tiny bit consoled Frank sometimes when I think that when the day comes
for me to leave Toddington there is not a single person I shall wish to say
goodbye to, even as a kid I was perfectly happy in a world of my own.
I have never made friends and I am more than thankful.

Will you be glad when we are married? I hate it, kid, when I think we
shall have to wait at least another twelve months and perhaps longer
than that before we can be married. I sometimes think I shall never have
my kiddie and I should want one awfully badly, we have both agreed
that we should, have we not? I shall want this baby because if afterwards
anything happened to you, I could always look at him and know he was
yours. Our baby, Frank, do you understand? Do you know how much
I love you when I think and write like this?

I must finish now sweetheart mine, please write to me and tell me you
love me.
My darling Frank!

Your very own wife, Nell

                                                            8 December 1915
My own dearest one,

I am sending you some Tobacco and Cigarettes, it is a fortnight since
I sent you the last, enclosed with the remainder of your underclothes.
Frank, tell me would you rather I sent tobacco and cigarettes to you every
week or is once a fortnight quite alright? You see darling, in sending once
a fortnight I send a double quantity and even so I do not know if the
amount I send is correct. I have asked you before about this, several times
in my letters to you I have mentioned it. Of course I know you like the
'Gold Flake', but I am not sure about the 'Richmond Gem'.

I posted you quite a long letter yesterday and I did think I would send
this parcel with no letter but I dare not kid because perhaps you would feel
a tiny bit disappointed, would you feel disappointed? Tell me please Frank.

I have been wondering how long the parcels take to reach you. Today is
the 8th, sixteen full days and then Christmas, you may get this parcel just

about the 25th. If so darling, with all the luck in the world and may you soon, very soon be home again.

Two and a half years I have known you Frank, and during some parts of the time I have been very happy, not always happy because it would not be possible for any woman who loves her particular man as I love you to be always happy, but have we not had some lovely times kid? You too have been happy, I feel sure you have. Frank you have told me that you have never repented of coming to Toddington, never repented loving me in the way you have done and still do. I used to be awfully frightened that you would one day feel sorry that you ever came here but I do not feel afraid now about it because I know you are always going to love me and one day marry me. Kid, darling, is it not too horrible having to wait? I want so badly to be married to you even if you had to go right back to the war the moment after we were married, I was going to say I should not mind but I think I should, you would have to creep away in the darkness in the very early morning, the next morning I mean, like you have done several times before from the Charing Cross Hotel, do you remember?

I must not write any more today because I have to stitch up your little box. I wanted a letter from you today but it has not arrived. I do not get many letters Frank, today is Wednesday and the last letter I got from you was Thursday last, of course I had the letter on Sunday, the one that had been delayed. I do not blame you my darling, I know it is not your fault. My husband goodbye,

Your very own, Nell

Sunday, 12 December and Monday, 13 December 1915

Frank, my dearest one,

I was quite disappointed this morning when there was no letter from you. I did so want one but I must not be greedy. I had a letter from you on Friday, thank you so much, thanks for all your letters Frank, they seem all I have to live for just now. I posted you yesterday, no I mean Saturday, I started this letter to you yesterday sweetheart but I could not finish it because some officer men belonging to the Northants Yeomanry came in for tea, but about the letter I posted you Saturday, I wonder what you will say kid. I should love to be near you when you open the letter, just a tiny bit of me sweetheart, unless my memory fails me you had used to be particularly fond of resting your head, well you know all about it, you know just where I mean.

I went to bed last night feeling very miserable. I have a beastly cold again but not quite so bad as the one I had in August, do you remember how frightfully miserable I was through dinner, I mean the last Saturday when I met you at the Charing Cross Hotel? I was very poorly and so unhappy about you going away, so were you kid, unhappy – you, if I remember rightly, sat and snuffled through dinner, poor old Frank dear, you have cried quite a lot about me one time or another have you not? Many times my darling. I have kissed your tears away and loved comforting you after I had made you unhappy.

I am not sure Frank but I may go to London tomorrow, I want to do some shopping, but today here is very cold, it has been snowing for about two hours, so it will really depend on how I feel about things in the morning, but I stay in until I hate the idea of going out, is it not too stupid?

Before I forget, Frank dear, I wonder when you will be coming home, but what I was going to say is, if when the time comes I do not get your wire in time to meet you at Folkestone or wherever you come to, you are to wait for me in London, of course I shall want awfully to meet you off the boat but in case that is quite impossible dearest I want you to know that I should hate in a way for you to come straight down here. No kid, I must see you, must have you all to myself for the first hours. You do understand Frank, my husband, how I feel about everything, do you not?

I am so unhappy about you sometimes but I think I really do very well in not getting more miserable under the circumstances, you must admit sweetheart that I have tried to manage and that I have done everything in my power to please you, not that I had to make myself do this but because it came to me in quite a natural sort of way, I suppose it is because I love you, because you are my man. Frank, are you glad that I think of you as my one man out of all the men in the world? Would you have it different supposing you could go back say three years, would you come over to Toddington on one particular Sunday morning in June and then keep on coming until the whole neighbourhood was more than interested, please tell me.

Write to me sweetheart and if I am not going away from home tomorrow no doubt I shall write you again, but in any case Wednesday dear without fail.

The coins were quite nice kid, thanks dear for suggesting the smaller ones for the kid's bracelet, but just at present she has not a suitable bracelet for them, I know what you will say, get her one, but no, Frank, not just now, shortly perhaps. I will take great care of the coins for you and later on perhaps she might like the smaller ones.
All my love dearest, and until I see you all my thoughts are for you my darling.

Your wife, Nell

16 December 1915

Frank, my own dearest,

A week tomorrow since I got your last letter, seven days kid is it not too bad? I just feel today as if I can't go on unless I do get your letters more often, I particularly feel so today because I am not well. I went up to Town Tuesday (I told you in my letter dear I thought of going did I not?) it was a beastly day really, quite a nice morning to start with and then rain at about 12 o'clock. I got rather fed up and miserable before I reached home. I missed you so much kid, I do not know if it was through going out but yesterday I had a most dreadful headache, and finished up the day with a terrific bilious attack, so that is why I did not write to you yesterday. I wanted to awfully badly, and I really do not feel much like writing today, although I am feeling better. You are quite right Frank, Mrs Bonner is awfully good to me when I am not well, and last night I did want a tiny bit of comforting. I am frightfully run down really sweetheart, do you know I am? I myself am not surprised, the last fifteen months of my life have been anything but comforting. I would not go through the time again, not for anything on earth.

How are you my darling, are you keeping quite well? I am anxious about you dearest because once having your letters from somewhere near Salonika, the delay now during the last six days worries me more than before. I cannot help feeling troubled, Frank, and there will always be this certain amount of unrest for me until we are married and then I shall keep you busy for a long time patching me up, making me quite well, I wonder if you would like doing this, or would you get rather tired? Tell me sweetheart. I love you very very much and not getting your letters makes such a difference.

Goodbye my husband until I write again.

Your very own, Nell

18 December 1915

Frank, my own darling,

I cannot understand I have had no letter yesterday or again today, eight days now since I last heard from you. I wonder if you are getting my letters kid, I hope you are even if I do not get yours, because I know Frank dear you would miss my letters, and you being right away out there darling would make the whole thing seem worse for you if you do not get letters, there are letters and letters are there not kid? But I mean if you did not get my letters. I am really miserable, I have been all the week. I am sure it is because I have not heard from you, and today my heart seems right down in my shoes.

I shall be so glad when this war is over and you are safely home once again. In the last letter I got from you, which was a topping letter Frank, you refer to one of my letters sweetheart and say something about the lovely bedroom we will have, quite a big one and awfully comfy, and just exactly as I want to have it. Thank you so much dearest. I know you will be a dear husband to me when that perfect time comes, we are going to be quite happy are we not? I do hope so – I love you so much that sometimes I am afraid that something will happen to prevent us from being married. It is no good kid, I shall never settle down again now until I have seen you. Sixteen weeks tomorrow since I last said goodbye to you and up to about a fortnight ago I managed fairly well but during this last week and no letters I just feel as if I must see you, as if I can make no further attempt to try and look on the bright side. Frank, when are you coming home? I want you to so badly.

Bob came home this morning for her Christmas holiday, she is looking awfully well, and so pleased, absolutely delighted to see me, she asked very nicely after you dear.

A week today Christmas Day, I shall be relieved when it is over. I am not sure if Bertie is coming home for Christmas, I pray God not, I asked him not to come home for it when he was last here.

My darling I am sending you tobacco and cigarettes next week, probably Monday, and I wonder if you would like me to send out papers to you? I think you said in one of your letters about a fortnight ago that you had not seen an English paper, tell me kid if you would like me to send them – is the 'Over Seas Daily Mail' any good?

I have not sent you papers, Frank, because I did not know if you would care for me to do so. I have asked you many times to tell me just what you want and it should be sent.

All my love my husband, all my thoughts my dear one. Write to me please Frank.

Your wife, Nell

25 December 1915

Frank, my own darling,

I am just going to write you a tiny letter and then pack up your tobacco and cigarettes. I feel I must send the parcel Frank dear, although there was no letter again this morning.

Christmas Day today and the whole of the day wet, teeming with rain. I do not remember just such a beastly day for Dec 25th. I am not really very miserable today but I have had to keep busy so that I did not think too much about not hearing from you. Sweetheart, I wonder why it is – of course, Frank, I cannot help wondering and the result is I get frightful headaches, but I shall soon hear shall I not dearest? I know it is not your fault. I do not think I should care so much if I knew for certain that you were not ill, but that is just uppermost in my mind the whole of the time, that you may be ill and wanting me because I feel sure, Frank, if you are ill then there would be sometimes [sic] when you would want me and I could make you so comfy could I not? and be perfectly happy watching you my darling.

Three Christmas Days I have known you now Frank dear and the whole three I have had to spend alone without you, I wonder where we shall all be this time next year, and what we shall be doing, perhaps it is quite as well we do not know, but I for one would love to have just a tiny peep into the future.

I have absolutely no news to tell you as nothing happens. I think sometimes you must find my letters uninteresting because darling all I seem to tell you in them is how much I love you and want you. I wish I could just write down on paper my feelings during the last fortnight, night and day, you would then perhaps understand (if when you come back you find my face full of lines and wrinkles) the cause of all the little crow's feet and all the beastly things that will appear in one's face when they are always troubled, when they are always wanting one particular thing knowing all the time there is a chance of it being taken away from them for always.

I must end up my darling, wishing you all the luck in the world and a tiny prayer to God tonight asking him for a letter tomorrow.

Your very own, Nell
P.S. Frank, I know you are writing to me, I am sure you are but I am not getting your letters and I feel afraid. Nell

30 December 1915

Frank, my own darling,

At last I have got three letters from you dated as follows, Dec 7th, 12th and 16th, all three arrived this morning, the last letter from you before these I received Dec 10th so you see darling I had not heard from you for nineteen whole days, your letter dated Dec 7th is headed 'Still in Hospital'. Frank my husband I am so sorry but I do not even know what you have been suffering from or why you were there. I could not understand the delay in your letters. I have been frightfully troubled but all I can say now dear is that I am glad you are better because in your letter of the 12th you say I am quite right again.

By the time this reaches you, you will know I have been bothered about your letters all through Christmas, you know kid I did not hear from you it was too dreadful, Frank, I was so unhappy.

You dearest of sweethearts, I started this letter just before lunch and then Mrs Bonner came along and said lunch was ready and we were just sitting down like two old women when your dear wire came, handed in yesterday at Salonica [sic]. Not bad really, kid, considering the distance and circumstances, thank you so much. I wonder which letter or parcel you had just received, was it the one dated Dec 11th? I do not really care which letter or parcel; you have made me very happy sweetheart. Frank dear, three letters and a telegram all on the same day, is it not topping? I shall be able now to go on for at least a time.

Please tell me in your reply to this about your dear self, tell me if you were very seedy when you were in the Hospital, and what was the matter? And how long were you there? Poor old Frank.

I do wonder if eventually you will get all my letters. I posted your first warm shirts etc. with letter dated Nov 5th, have you received this? And then a letter Nov 11th and 15th Nov, 24th and a letter I believe in between 15th and 24th. When you do write to me, Frank dear, please give me the dates of my letters as you receive them. I particularly wish to know if you have received both parcels of underclothing.

Thank you my darling for the £10 cheque in one of your letters this morning, it is awfully good of you Frank. Of course dear you do know I could not stay on here without your help, that was an understood thing between us was it not, before you left England. The whole matter of paying bothers me now but I do appreciate your kindness, you know I do, and later on when we are married and one day we may be well off we shall think of these times of wriggling through with occasional payments.

Goodbye sweetheart mine, I love you, please tell me when will you try to get home. I posted tobacco and cigarettes to you Tuesday last, the 28th. All my love dearest,

Your wife, Nell
P.S. Please send Thomson a cheque for the enclosed account.

3 January 1916

Frank, my own darling,

I am afraid it is going to be rather beastly in this house in trying to manage without Mrs Bonner. She really left me last Tuesday but has been in once or twice since then to help, this week her husband is home so I do not suppose I shall see very much of her, which in a way is rather a nuisance because I must go down to Bedford very shortly to shop for Bob, her wants in the way of clothes this time seem endless but no doubt I shall get through, but I really do think that I shall not have quite so much time for writing to you as I have had. Will you mind very much my darling if you do not get quite so many letters from me, it would make no difference, Frank, I shall always be thinking about you, loving you and waiting for you to come back.

Sweetheart mine I have not heard from you since I last wrote to you – today is Monday and the last letters that I got from you was on Thursday last week, the same day that I got your dear wire. Of course I may hear tomorrow or I may have to wait a long time again, I trust not.

Mrs Cross has left Toddington. She came in to say goodbye to me one day last week, she told me she was going to stay for a week with the Doctor who is now at Wendover and then she is going into a boarding house in London, somewhere near Regents Park. Mr & Mrs Schelesman have also gone away and the Griffin Hotel at the present time is closed. The Schelesmans were going back to their Flat in Town, at least she said so. I should think it is a case of great uncertainty as to where they have gone.

Frank dearest, do you remember the night we went over there, Tommy, yourself and I, or rather do you remember coming back from there just when we crossed over the road? Tell me if you do remember please, Frank, in your next letter, and then following on this the night we were all three in Town. I wanted so badly to come to you after you had left the Hotel Russell, perhaps I did not realise at the time the cause of me being more than ready to row with Tommy on this particular night but I very soon found out how I felt about everything when I got back to Toddington. I wonder, kid, only supposing I had come round to your rooms what would have happened, should I have been sent away again or would you have taken hold of me and held me in the way you have done since, just in that particular way, Frank, that I am starving for now when nothing else seems to matter in the whole world.

You say when you come back just at first you will be quite mad. I do not mind my husband, I shall be too intensely happy, you can do with me just as you like.

Goodbye my darling, I will write to you again very soon.

Always sweetheart,

Your very own, Nell
P.S. The enclosed received from Bertie this morning. 'Some estrangement.'

R.E. Barracks
Currah Camp
Dear Nell,

Very sorry to trouble you but will you please send me on my snaffle bridle with nose band of bridle in taproom, also zasps (?) out of box in saddle room.

Might be going to the front shortly, shall have some things to send back, where shall I send them to Longhurst & Skinner's.

Yrs, Bertie
P.S. Please give my love to Bobbie. If you have got a photo of yourself to send me should be very pleased as I don't suppose we shall see each other for some time, if again. B.A.

9 January 1916
Frank, my own darling,

Please forgive me in not writing to you for several days, five whole days
I believe. I am sorry, Frank, but I will try dear to make up for it this
coming week, it was really not my fault and knowing that I have not
been able to write to you has bothered me quite a lot. You see sweetheart
I have had a large amount of needlework for Bob, and then Wednesday
and Thursday the Engineers from Houghton Regis were out on a scheme
and of course once again made this house their Headquarters. Yesterday,
Saturday, I went down to Bedford with Bob shopping, went on the 9.16
train from Harlington and returned on the 6.15 from Bedford, quite a
long day but it was really very nice, and tomorrow, sweetheart, Bob and
I are going to London, but I must explain to you about this. In the first
instance I have promised to take her for such a long time now, and when
I told her what you had said in your letter about buying her a small
present for the New Year she immediately said she would like to go to
London so for tomorrow night I have booked two stalls at the Palace, the
Revue Bric a Brac that is on there is supposed to be very good and we are
going by the 11.53 train from Harlinton [sic] and return by the 12.5 from
St Pancras and drive of course from Luton, so Frank dearest I will write
you again on Tuesday and tell you how we got on.

   I shall think about you kid when I am sitting in the Palace, this
time I shall not be quite alone, do you remember? I never could quite
understand how you expected I should come round to the Palace that
particular night, I certainly did not expect to find you there, I think
perhaps if I had known I should not have come I should have gone
elsewhere but I shall never quite forget how I felt when walking down the
gangway I first caught sight of you, I simply had to make myself walk
on and when I sat down in the chair I could hardly breathe and then
the man just in front (with a woman that was awfully well dressed) the
persistent way he had of turning round and staring, not forgetting the
good looking man that appeared to be waiting for someone just outside
the Palace. This was when I was coming away but it was no good,
I was too unhappy, I wanted nobody in the whole world, not even you
sweetheart – it is the only time that is stamped on my memory of not

wanting you. I could have made you unhappy that night, Frank, if I had cared to do so but I am glad now, more than glad my darling that I did not do so.

I have had your letters on the last two Wednesdays, Dec 29th and Jan 5th. I wonder if this means that I am only going to get your letters once a week, even so I suppose I shall have to be satisfied and as you said in one of your letters it cannot be for so very long now. I love you so much Frank darling and tomorrow when I am in Town I shall think of you dozens of times, I am looking forward tremendously to the time when you will be home on leave, we will have a perfect time will we not Frank? Not even the tiniest of rows my darling? Please keep on writing to me quite often. All my love my dearest one,

Your wife, Nell

11 January 1916

Frank, my own darling,

According to [my] promise dear, I am writing to you Tuesday to tell you about our day in Town yesterday, Bob and I had quite an enjoyable day really or rather half a day. The train as you no doubt remember gets to St Pancras at about 1.8. We went straight away to Frascatti's [sic] for lunch, had a look round the shops in the afternoon and then tea at the Piccadilly Tea Room which was crowded, absolutely full, when we left there we sauntered back up Regent Street, bought some chocolates at Fuller's, more shop windows and then walked very slowly back to Frascatti's [sic] for dinner upstairs which the kid enjoyed immensely, leaving there for the Palace at 8 o'clock. We found the show there awfully good, left the Palace at about 11.15 and walked back to St Pancras, had lots of time to spare for the 12.5 train out, Fleckney met us at Luton with one of his charming governess carts (we had specially ordered an open conveyance as we wanted to get some fresh air) and then home, both of us feeling rather tired, we came into the house by the side door and along the passage and there fixed in the candlestick was your dear letter dated Dec 20th. Thank you so much Frank darling,

I was awfully please[d] to get it, for me it finished up the day with one of the happiest of endings, it is quite the first time I have sat on my bed and read one of your letters at 2 o'clock in the morning, this was of course before even taking off my hat and coat and then after I was in bed with my hair down just all ready for sleep I had to read it again, again thank you so much my husband.

You appear to be getting my letters quite well Frank, there are one or two (which should have reached by or before Dec 20th) you have not acknowledged yet but no doubt you will get them, you have received all those that were redirected to you from France. I am still anxious about your second lot of underclothes, this was sent to you Nov 24th, directed to you dear at Salonica [sic].

Dearest, in the letter I got from you last night you did not mention about your leave, have you no idea sweetheart as to when this will be? Again referring to your letter of yesterday you say you are a wee bit piggy about that never to be forgotten day in London Nell, 'pardon me Sir', not one day but two, dear old Frank it is a real shame to keep on reminding you of your beastly behaviour and when you come home on leave we will really square up the thing for always. That is of course if you are very good, but do you know my darling I have forgiven you long ago.

I do want you to come home Frank, want you to help and advise me in many ways. The kid thanks you for her day in Town, she thinks the whole thing was wonderful.

Goodbye my dearest one, I love you.

Your wife, Nell

                                                                21 January 1916

Frank, my own darling,

I am certainly not getting many letters from you. I received one letter on Jan 5th and another Jan 10th, since then I have not heard, two letters in nearly three weeks Frank dear, not many, ay kid? I just wait every morning for the postman hoping against hope that there will be a letter from you and then when I find there is not one I feel frightfully miserable.

I just feel as if I cannot bother to dress to go down and start one more weary day, my God Frank this is a damned forsaken hole.

Day after day I just keep on wondering when I shall see you again, keep on wondering what this year is going to bring forth and where I shall be this time next year. I hope and pray that I shall be with you absolutely Frank darling for good, but at the same time I am not anyways certain about this because this dreadful War appears to me to have no end, but as I have said before, when you come home we can make final arrangements.

I have no news sweetheart; the kid returns to school a week today, Jan 24th. I have been awfully busy this holiday getting through some needlework for her, but I am nearly finished now. I am afraid I have got rather merry over it, you see really I get very little time for sewing but I have managed to get quite a bit finished. My darling I wonder if you are keeping quite well after your rheumatism, is it not a nuisance about your letters, you do write to me oftener than once a week Frank do you not? I love you so much and when I do not hear from you, well you understand my dearest one, you know exactly how you feel when you do not hear from me. I feel just the same, I must do, because as I have said I love you so much and live for you absolutely, and as you say in your letter, however wearying the time may be please wait for me. Yes, I will wait for you my husband because you are my one man.

I must finish up now Frank dear and I will try to write to you more often this week but I do want your letters so badly. I am feeling quite fit kid. Goodbye darling, with all my love and all the luck in the world.

Your wife, Nell

21 January 1916

Frank, my own darling,

I just feel as if I must write to you. I have no news to tell you but there are times Frank when I feel as if I must write and by sitting down and just doing so I feel better and I am sure less lonely.

It is such a beastly day here today, raining and so frightfully dull. I have not had a letter from you sweetheart either yesterday or today and

as I told you in my letter posted [to] you Monday I had only received two
letters in three weeks, just too jolly bad is it not kid? Bob had a letter from
you yesterday, it had been redirected from Howard College. The letter is
dated Dec 5th and received here Jan 18th, six weeks and two days. Hope
and trust I have not to wait that length of time for my letter, if so I do
not think it will arrive in time, I shall have gone to my grave worried
absolutely to death about you my darling.

I could not finish this letter yesterday and Frank darling the whole
situation is saved – your letters have arrived, five for me and one for
the kid. Mine are Dec 29th and 31st, Jan 1st 3rd and 5th the last three are
numbers 1, 2 and 3 and sweetheart for all of them thank you so much.
I think it is a good idea about the numbering of your letters, yes Frank
please do number them. I shall [do] as you say then know if I get them
all. Bob also had a letter from you yesterday but I have just told you this
have I not? It was the one thanking her for the photograph. She was very
pleased and I believe, kid, she has already replied to your letter. Yes dear,
I too thought her photograph postcards quite good, we had such fun the
day she had them taken, she could hardly remember being photographed
before and she was really quite funny about it, she keeps on growing
Frank and widening out but one can hardly be surprised as really she
seems to think of nothing else besides eating and occasionally loving me
but when you do see her you will see a vast difference in her, I think she is
improving and I should say when she gets to be about 18 or 19 she will be
more or less like the side of a house.

You appear to be getting my letters quite well dear, although my letters
are like yours in arriving all out of order. I think there was one dated Nov
27th which you do not seem to have mentioned, but perhaps by now you
have received it.

You ask me in your letter, the one dated Jan 1st, about Christmas and
the New Year – you say tell me all about it. I couldn't Frank, honestly
kid there is nothing to tell, it was all very ordinary and uninteresting,
New Year's Eve I remember we were all in bed by 10.15, perhaps you will
not believe me, Frank dear, but night after night we do not get one single
person in with the exception [of] Flo Potts, and dear old Will, the man
who is kind enough to pump up the water. I had rather a nice card from
Ethel Rawkins at Christmas, I think I will send it on to you for you to see.

Re. one of your other letters, where you speak of the glorious Turkish and Persian rugs and our home, you sweet darling as you say perhaps I should not think very much of some of your schemes and I should say yes or no, but would it not be top hole my darling just arranging, I am so glad my dearest one that it makes you happy to think about our future home and all the lovely times we are going to have when we are married, I too love thinking about it.

Goodbye my darling, my husband,

Your very own, Nell

23 January 1916

Frank, my own dearest one,

I received another letter from you this morning dated Jan 10th and numbered 6, so numbers 4 and 5 are still to arrive, thank you so much, Frank, it is a topping letter and made me feel so jolly happy after reading it. I have not very much time today for a long letter because I have been busy packing for Bob, she returns to school tomorrow, Monday, but I thought dear if I did not write you today I should not be able to do so until Tuesday and I do not like keeping you waiting so long for a letter.

My own darling, yes, you are quite right, the cigarettes that you speak of that were tied up with the wee blue ribbon, I did have them in my hand and just kissed them as they laid there feeling sure my darling that if not all, perhaps one or two you would smoke that my lips had touched. I have been awfully anxious to know if you would remark about this particular tiny bundle. I too thought the ribbon very pretty.

Frank dearest, I promise you not to leave Toddington until after you have been home on leave but I really do seem to be getting deeper and deeper into debt even with your help and you have indeed been good to me. I do not know how I am going to manage but this month I always think is a dreadful month for settling up accounts and the kid of course is a great expense just now but as I have said before, not until I have seen you and been advised by you will I make the slightest attempt at getting out.

My husband, yes, I will write to you quite often and not wait until
I get your letters but have not done so Frank, I have kept on writing to
you. In your letter today you thank me for my letter of Dec 8th with the
Tobacco and Cigarettes, also for my letter written on 24th but darling
I posted you a letter Nov 27th also Dec 7th the 11th and 12th, these I am
certain of and I may have sent others, but I think from today dear I will
number my letters to you starting with this letter as No. (1).

I thought this morning when I first read your letter that you were a
Shi[t] (I am not sure perhaps there are two t's) in wanting me to send
tobacco etc. to you every week, but just now I am loving you quite a lot
and I think I will consider it and if my decision is favourable I will post
you a very small quantity on Tuesday next.

I must really finish now my darling or I shall miss the post. Goodbye
sweetheart mine, I love you.

Your wife, Nell

27 January 1916

My own darling,

Frank dear, I said in my last letter to you which was Sunday that I would
post your tobacco etc. Tuesday but I could not do so sweetheart because
I have been rather hung up over Barkers account, but I am posting you
Tobacco and Cigarettes etc. today and please forgive me kid in keeping
you rather a long time for them.

I am so glad, up to now I have received your letters, the number ones,
I mean Nos. 1, 2, 3, 4, 5, 6 and 7. Of course they did not arrive in this
order but that does not matter as long as I get them. In your last letter
dear, No. 7, you say, by the way did you get the cheque sent in December,
yes Frank I did, on December 30th it reached here and on the same day
I wrote thanking you for it, and telling you how much I appreciated your
kindness. I have had the Devil's own job in paying this month I really
have felt frightfully worried at all times, you see, darling, Durance has
not settled up yet, if he had done so I should be much more comfortable.
I had a letter from him Dec 14th last saying if at all possible he would

settle by January 25th but up to the present I have not heard again from
him so if I get time I am writing to him tonight.

Today I do not feel worried and I am awfully fit and well.

Poor old Frank darling and is it really so very cold where you are?
I am so sorry for you. Yes, I had heard the tale about the small boy and
the Periscope but I never could quite imagine you feeling like the Nurse
(she hadn't one), of course it may be very different out there, but speaking
from experience I always found you had one when at home and a very
satisfactory one at that, with the exceptions (which were many) of when he
overstepped the mark and by so doing caused serious trouble. I wish to God
it could happen tonight, there is nothing in the whole world I should like
better, just you, my husband, just in your arms, Frank, in that particular
position I love frightfully, do you agree with me, do you think you would be
able to? Tell me because I love you my own dearest one.

I will send on your Spurs dear if possible early next week with your
Café au Lait, also notepaper, not forgetting more tobacco and cigarettes.
Goodbye my darling, once again take great care of yourself for my sake.
All my love is yours, just everything I have, my dearest one are you not?

Your wife, Nell

29 January 1916

No (3). The letter with the Tobacco should be No. 2, rather a nasty
number, but I really believe I forgot to put the tiny little 2 in the corner.
Yours, Nell

My own dearest sweetheart,
Five months today since I last saw you. 22 weeks really, what a long time.
Frank, has it seemed a weary waiting to you, to me I could not explain.

Thank you so much my darling for sending on the scorched envelope
for me to see, what an astonishing thing, I was awfully interested. Do
you know a letter came from you yesterday dated 16.1.16 and should have
been numbered 9 but there was no number, how dare you forget. I have
had quite a nice lot of letters from you this week, thank you Frank dear,

they have been awfully nice letters and I know you love me – how could you possibly write letters to me like you do if you did not mean every tiny word you say in them.

You say please tell me sweetheart what you do on Sunday afternoons when the place is closed, and now that it is Winter and no one disturbing you. There is very little to tell my darling, it is ages since we had a fire in the bottom room, Rose starts the fire in the C. Room and then after lunch or rather after 2.30 I pull up the couch quite near the fire and then fetch down my rug and eiderdown, pillow and not forgetting my tiny shawl and then with a book but first of all a cigarette (I am drifting into a confirmed smoker – I wonder what you will say, do you mind very much?) I have quite a comfy time for about two hours and often have nice sleeps, of course this is not always because sometimes I write to you quite long letters on Sunday afternoons.

I have not missed Mrs Bonner very much, really Frank I believe I am quite glad she has gone. One consolation, I have not got her to pay, neither has she to be kept, of course I find a little extra to do but not much. Rose is quite a good girl. I wonder when you will get this letter sweetheart because I have been thinking about your birthday. I am afraid you may not get this letter quite by then but I shall think of you on February 13th, think of you just a tiny bit extra if this is at all possible, and may you spend your next birthday under much happier circumstances to those of this year.

I am not sending you a present because I haven't any money, but you will not mind and you will quite understand, but I do so want you to know I have not forgotten the date so perhaps I will send this letter through to you registered so that it does not get lost, with all my love my husband and the best of luck for your birthday.

Goodbye my own darling, I love you so much today, but I always love you. One more Saturday night here which, thank God, will soon be over and then to bed, worse luck by one's self which I hate <u>because I want you</u> Frank dearest.

Your wife, Nell

Frank, my own darling,

I am writing to you again today although I sent you a long letter
yesterday but I know you would hate to open the parcel and find no
letter, because once before you told me you would have been very very
disappointed but please understand <u>Franklin</u> today this is going to be a
short letter as I really must give Rose a hand with the work. Enclosed
with this letter in box is your Café au Lait, Tobacco, Cigarettes, Spurs,
extra tabs and straps, 2 pairs of leather boot laces and last but not least
a most ferocious looking tin opener which I expect you will smile over
when you come across it. The laces dear you did not ask me to send but
I thought when I saw them in Fox's you might find them handy, also the
tin opener I thought if you had nothing to hand with which to open your
Café au Lait you would bless me in sending this one, but Frank after
buying the confounded thing from Brownings (you know, dear, the corner
shop) I thought it was not sufficiently sharp for cutting through tin, so of
course I had to ask dear old Kim Horley to sharpen it for me and here it
is all very beautiful. Please say thank you Nell darling for all the trouble
you have taken.

   Now about your dear self, how are you my sweetheart, are you keeping
well? I hope you are Frank. I am feeling really awfully fit. You said in
one of your letters you thought perhaps you were safer in 'Somewhere
near Salonica [sic] than in England', I wonder if you really are darling?
I see by this morning's paper there was another Air Raid last night by
Six Zeppilins [sic], no particulars really given, just states Bombs on
Eastern, North Eastern, and Midland Counties, very dreadful is it not,
kid, but I suppose it is all a part of this huge War. Again by the papers
things appear to be getting on the move where you are, but at the same
time the papers are extremely contradictory, one can hardly believe
what one reads. When the fighting does really start in or near Salonica
[sic] I shall be truly worried my husband, about you, more worried I am
sure than I have been up to the present. God knows some days even now
I worry and work myself into an absolute fever about you before I go to
bed and then I cannot get off to sleep for hours and hours. I love you so
much Frank and I want to be married to you so badly, I mean married

to you just this very minute. I hate waiting, but I will wait for you my darling because I firmly believe in the long run I shall have you and be absolutely satisfied.

Only six sheets again and this letter was to be quite short but it is to you, which makes all the difference in the world, so now my husband with all my love I must finish.

Your wife Nell

P.S. In my letter of yesterday I fully explained to you about your Spur straps and Frank dear I am enclosing your Nutta. I have had rather a difficulty in getting the Extra Tan, do you prefer this colour, tell me in your reply to this.

Goodbye darling, Nell

4 February 1916   Number 6

Frank, my own dearest one,

Many thanks for your letter dear No. 13 received yesterday, No. 12 is still to arrive, you say many thanks for your letter of the 3rd of January – is it not a nuisance Frank about the letters because letters dated as follows Dec 7th, 11th, 12th and 25th you, up to the time of writing your last letter to me, had not received and of course you should have done. I am awfully sorry my darling because I really do write to you quite a lot and I am going to keep on doing so.

Now first of all I am just going to contradict part of my Jan 3rd letter and emphasize more strongly my letter of Jan 29th as to Mrs Bonner having left me. I am not really the tiniest bit sorry she has gone, just the first day or two seemed beastly but we were busy in the house and I do not think I was feeling up to much. Bertie had not been gone away long if you remember, but anyway there the thing remains, even if Mrs Bonner wanted to come back now I would not have her and I am jolly glad I was beastly rude to you some time ago when we argued the point about her leaving me and that I should miss her so much because even then I was quite right, I do not to any great extent miss her, I think she is more sorry than I in having left here.

Dearest, today is Friday and on Tuesday last I posted your parcel. I wonder if you will have got it by the time this letter reaches you but what I was going to say is, darling, that I did not enclose your notepaper – there was not sufficient room in the box for it, but I will send it with your tobacco next week.

Rose and I were in bed last night by 9.45 with of course the place closed. I went straight off to sleep and slept soundly until Rose brought up my hot water this morning at about a ¼ to 8 and even then I did not want to get up, as I have already told you in one or two of my letters we get so few people in that I get absolutely bored stiff by bedtime. Take yesterday, for instance, Rose and I had tea at 4 o'clock and then during the evening Anderson strolled in, then Flo Potts and to finish up at 8.30 Dick Hunt, Frank dear no one else, just those three people for the whole evening. The time drags and drags, some nights I think it never will be 10 o'clock and when I finally go to bed I just think for his sake I am staying on here, for your sake Frank, because you have asked me to do so and because I love you as I have never loved anyone else, and I know my darling that it is terrible for you out where you are and I feel very very sorry for you, but when you come home, if only for your leave, we will be happy, so happy my darling because as you say in your letter I am your wife all but in name, thank you so much my husband your letters make me feel almost happy, just as happy as I can ever be without you.
With all my love.
Always my darling,

Your very own, Nell

6 February 1916   Sunday afternoon

My own dearest Frank,

Please note what I am doing this afternoon, as not very long ago you asked me to tell you all about my Sunday afternoons. I have not heard from you since I last wrote to you, which was on Friday, but I do not mind sweetheart, at least not very much because just lately I have had quite a number of letters from you and after I have heard from you I always feel as if I can go on again for a time.

Yesterday, here, was rather a depressing day and towards the evening I got a little down in the mouth. I wanted to see you so much Frank, there are some days and nights when I feel as if I am absolutely starving for you and when I go upstairs to bed I just look at your photograph (the full figure one), look at it for quite a long time and say 'Frank darling'!! And to me in just those two words is everything, but you know exactly how much I love you so as you feel sorry for yourself so you can feel sorry for me, there are times when I feel as if I can't go on unless I see you very soon but I am awfully brave really Frank and, as you say, I do try to keep a stiff upper lip but at times it is frightfully difficult, far more so than I ever imagined it could be.

Still no news in the village dear. One more Saturday night over thank God, I am always awfully glad to get to bed on Saturday nights because I always think it is one more Saturday nearer to seeing you. Frank, my darling, can you imagine what it will really be like when we do meet again, I for one will hardly know what to do. I am quite sure I shall feel strange and almost suffocated. Do you remember the first time I met you in London, after you had left here I mean, dear, I was full of nerves and perhaps not quite so sure of you then as I am now because I am sure of you Frank dearest, sure that one day you will marry me and very very soon too I hope.

But we have had some lovely weekends in Town have we not? We have both been very happy. I love you very much today my darling and tonight when I go to bed I shall wish with all my heart that you were going to be there to cuddle me up if only for a tiny minute, tell me, do you think you could if I asked you very very nicely?
Goodbye my dearest of all men, please keep on writing to me.
I love you.

Your wife, Nell

8 February 1916   Number 8

Frank, my own darling,

I received your 15th letter yesterday, the one posted on the 26th of January, Nos 12 and 14 are still to arrive. You are quite right kid where you say in your letter 'I cannot for the life of me understand what happens to the blessed mail', I have given it up absolutely as a bad job. Sometimes I do think we get all the letters eventually but I am damned if I know, please tell me in your reply to this have you received my letters dated as follows Dec 7th, 11th, 12th and 25th? I do hope you have Frank dear. I particularly wanted you to receive the one written on the 11th, in this letter I had accepted your bet about Mrs Horace Fletcher re. your letter dated Nov 17th where you say that you will lay me two to one in sovereigns that Mrs H. Fletcher produces a baby Fletcher within twelve months. I also said that I thought it would be quite wise for you to send along your two sovereigns at once as I always thought it much safer for someone to hold the money. Again referring to this letter I enclosed a tiny bit of myself tied up with blue silk, when it left here it was a sweet little curl, of course from my head I mean, you know how curly my hair is do you not? Frank darling, but tell me sweetheart have you received my letters as dated?

I was awfully pleased to get your letter yesterday and to read what you say – that you have heard on good authority you will probably be going back to France in about a month. I am not going to believe it Frank, to me, it sounds much too good to be true. I shall just wait for your cable.

Yes darling, I do remember the night we came back from Bedford and you are quite right it was not Ampthill Show Day and of course I know which day you mean, we had been down to Bedford Theatre to see 'The Belle of New York'. Before going there we had dinner at The Embankment Hotel and then coming home if you remember the man 'Rowe' that was driving lost his way, and how about the drive home, I like your style Frank where you say I was rather tired and wanted making a wee bit of fuss of, I remember sometimes when you have looked at me I have heard the word lascivious but I think if I remember rightly it was not me that night, you were 'It' absolutely.

I posted you some tobacco etc. Dec 28th, the letter enclosed in this parcel was dated Dec 25th, have you received it? Please tell me, since then

I have posted two parcels, Jan 27th and Feb 1st, and I am sending you tobacco again this week, also your notepaper no doubt Thursday, dear, and then I shall write to you again.

Goodbye my dearest, I love you in just the same way as I have always done. My one man, my husband.

Always your very own, Nell

10 February 1916   Number 9

Frank, my own darling,

Re. my letter of Tuesday I am sending your tobacco etc. today and I hope you will get it quite quickly. I have not heard from you darling since Monday, I rather hoped there would be a letter this afternoon but no luck, your number 12 and 14 letters are still to arrive, I told you this in my last letter. I wonder what's happened to them? I really cannot think of the tiniest bit of news to tell you darling, this place is most dreadfully quiet and just at the present time I do not think there is a scandal of any description, they are evidently waiting until you come home and then they will be awfully busy.

There are very few people that ask me about Bertie now. I think at last they have begun to grasp that by so doing they are treading on very thin ice. Of course just a few specially ask after him but I feel so uncomfortable when they do, Frank, I hate it, I shall be so glad, so altogether relieved when the whole thing is settled, when I belong to him no longer, there are some times, sweetheart, when I feel my position most keenly, but you must know Frank my darling how very unsatisfactory the whole thing is, you do do you not, darling? And you will as soon as it is in your power take me away and marry me. I know you will, but I do get so tired of waiting, tired of living on here.

You were awfully funny kid in your last letter about the festive farmers playing 'shell out' where you say their shell out always makes one grin because that is the very last thing they want to do, you are right sweetheart, it is indeed the very last thing they want to do, what a lot they are, Frank, when one thoroughly weighs them up, in every way I mean. Just fancy any woman (no matter what her age might be) being married to either Attwood, Anderson or John Hunt, and what a revelation to them if only once in their lives they could love a woman as you have loved me, but no they could not, they do not understand, but dearest there are not many people about that love each other quite in the same way as we do, do you agree with me in this? I know you do, I am quite right am I not?

Goodbye my dearest, I love you.

Your wife, Nell

17 February 1916   Number 11

My own darling,

Frank dear, now I am going to give you a damned big slating, first of all when the devil are you going to send my next cheque? I seem to have waited such a long time for it and there are one or two accounts I must pay, perhaps you have sent the cheque and I have not received it because in your No. 7 letter dated 12.1.16 you say 'I shall be sending you a cheque in a day or two', and now for further slating I received three letters from you this morning No's 18, 19, 20. Number nineteen letter was really not numbered but I could see by the three dates that it should be nineteen. The first two letters, 18 and 19, just full of grumbling about not hearing from me. I can't help it, all I know is that I keep on writing to you a jolly sight oftener than you write to me, this I am quite sure of, so if you do not get them Frank please do not blame me, now I have finished with the slating part of the programme, only please in the future do not forget to number your letters because I think the idea quite good, we really ought to have thought of it before, Frank.

My darling, up to the time of your writing your last letter to me you really do seem to have received all my letters and parcels with the exception of the three letters in December, dates as follows Dec 7th, 11th and 12th. Of course sweetheart I quite understand how you feel when you do not hear from me. I too feel just in the same way when your letters are a long time coming, I just feel as if there is nothing to live for and that

I cannot carry on. I am not really feeling very happy today, I cannot help it, the whole thing is not very satisfactory is it Frank dear? Some days of course I look upon it in a more hopeful sort of way, but at all times no matter how I feel I just know that I love you in that mad sort of passionate way where there is no going back, no half ways about it.

I just belong to you Frank my husband, body and soul for you to do with me just as you will. No darling, I have not heard from Bertie since I last wrote to you about him. I enclosed a letter of his to you did I not? For this I am extremely thankful, I do not want to hear from him.

Yes, I am awfully glad kid about you coming back nearer to Salonica [sic] and as you say dear, now that the weather is going to buck up you will perhaps be alright. I hope and trust you will keep fit my darling, I want you to because I love you so much.

Feb 1st I posted you a parcel containing your spurs etc. I am anxious to know if they are quite alright, by the time this letter reaches you, you will perhaps have replied telling me all about them.

Yes I know all about it, I have heard tales like that before. Did you say he stuck his off fore into a hole or did you say for God's sake send out to me a large quantity of cobbler's wax? Poor old Frank, I am so glad you were not hurt, how unfortunate for you darling.

I must finish up now dear, I am feeling much brighter than when I first started writing so you see darling the result of writing to you. I love you, Frank, and I am so glad you want me. Please keep on always wanting me.

Your wife, Nell

21 February 1916   Number 13

My own darling,

Frank dear, I am feeling most awfully jealous about you today, please do not think me altogether too foolish will you? but I want you to tell me all about the women you meet out there, I cannot help feeling jealous sometimes because I love you so much and last night (Sunday) after supper I just sat on and thought about you for quite a long time and cried a tiny bit. I was unhappy, Frank, and when I got up to bed so very cold

[I] shivered absolutely right through. In the last letter that I got from you, you say that because you love me and want me so much you have kept dead straight in every way and you mean that Frank, it is true every word of it, is it not?

Darling, I cannot quite explain to you what I mean but there are women out there are there not, that you could go to see if you felt so inclined and now that you are back in Salonica [sic], Frank, forgive me and tell me all about it, perhaps I am not quite fair to you in questioning you about this, but if you really knew how much I love you, you will understand and you do belong to me, you are mine, my very own and I can ask you all about these things that mean so much to me.

I had Bob's weekly letter yesterday and she tells me she has heard from you, thank you so much dear for writing to her, she was very delighted, she also told me she had received a letter from Tommy, his address now is Staff J.O.C.

Yeomanry Brigade

Western Frontier Force

Mersa Matruk

Base M.E.F

<u>Alexandria</u>

Please explain to me Staff J.O.C. – what does it mean? I had not cried for quite a long time until last night, but I wanted you to be here so badly or I wanted to be with you just wherever you were, if I could only have looked at you and stroked your hair, it would not be true if I said that would be sufficient, it would not suffice, I have waited for you so long now that it must be all or nothing.

I often think about your hair Frank, how is it looking now darling? It was always very lovely, do you have to keep it quite short? Or is it quite natural now as it used to be I mean?

I was awfully amused in the kid's letter yesterday – after speaking about your letter to her she says 'Mama dear I hope you sent him a cable for his birthday as I told you to but I do not suppose you forgot you dear sweet thing', so when I write to her I shall have to (forget) I mean admit to having forgotten about the cable but I think it was nice of her to have remembered your birthday. I too remembered sweetheart, did I not in my letters to you.

I posted your last lot of tobacco etc. Saturday last, the 19th, have you received it? Goodbye my dear husband.
With all my love,

Always your own, Nell
P.S. Thanks, dear, I have received the receipt from Thomson's

24 February 1916   Number 14

Frank, my own darling,

A week today since I last heard from you, last Thursday. I did get your letter number 17 the next day on the Friday but I am not counting that one as it ought to have arrived before, a week seems so long Frank to wait but I do not think there has been any letters for anyone today, not up to the present. It was snowing on and off the whole of yesterday and during the night a very heavy snow must have fallen because this morning it was quite twelve inches in depth and is still snowing, some people say anything for a change but personally I abhor snow.

I am sending you three 'Daily Mirrors' today, I thought perhaps you might like to see the sketches of the boxing, I think they are not really bad. I am also sending you the 'London Magazine'. I did not know if the 'Seven Years at the German Court' would interest you.

I really have no news Frank but I never have, have I kid? I have apologised to you before because of my uninteresting letters, and the reply I always get from you is keep on writing kid, so what am I to do?

Frank darling, do you remember when Connie Burton left here she went home to help look after her mother who was very ill, well her mother Mrs Burton died last Sunday, and I understand knowing it to be true that Connie is pregnant. Is it not too dreadful, Frank, when one thinks that her mother died knowing of this girl's condition. I feel in a way really sorry for Connie because whoever the man may be, he can have no intention of marrying her, or if so he would [have] married her before, if only to have satisfied her mother. I understand the man is a clerk in Swaffields office at Ampthill.

I do wonder if there will be a letter for me this afternoon, a week is a long time is it not? But I have got more used now to the uncertainty of your letters arriving that I do not mind quite so much, but it would indeed be delightful to be able to expect them every day like I had used to do.

Before I forget, in one of the Mirrors I am sending you there is a sketch of part of the result of one of the Air Raids on Salonica. I thought you specially would like to see that one, tell me.

You poor darling, and you have had such a lot of this dreadful weather have you not? Today here is rather terrible and to make matters worse there is quite a wind and at the same time freezing and only to think sweetheart perhaps you have had months of it. I feel sorry for you, Frank, and if you only live to come through, which I hope and pray to God you may, next Winter we may be in our own home and then it may snow, rain or freeze just whatever it likes, I should not mind, would you? In just the room that we have spoken of so many times, the huge fire, two lovely chairs and just a very low flat hassock sort of thing where I could sit right down near you, because I could read for hours if I had one of your hands just touching me.

Can you imagine all this, do you sometimes love to think about it, to picture our home where I am going to be so happy with you my husband.

I must finish now dear, with all the love I am capable of, always the same. I love you.

Your wife-to-be, Nell

26 February 1916   Number 15

My own dearest one,

Your registered letter of the 12th Feb No. 22 came yesterday, many many thanks for it Frank dear and the enclosure, also your £20 cheque was more than acceptable, I really have been awfully troubled about money matters during January and this month but now darling thanks to you I shall be able to manage for a time, you are very good to me Frank. I was awfully pleased to hear you got my 29th of January letter in time for your birthday, you say it is just 10 o'clock Nell and in 2 hours I shall be 31.

Frank, you are a damned cheat, I am sure it is 32, and I am surprised at
you trying to sneak off 12 months, you can say as you jolly well like but
I shall believe just what I think.

Yes, I do know what you mean my sweetheart and that perhaps
I should have another quite black bruise somewhere, I have heard it called
by a good many names but never before 'Somewhere' but seriously Frank
I was quite frightened when it happened, and I believe you were too, but
knowing now your ravenous appetite, when you come home on leave you
will not be allowed such liberties.

The weather is still very dreadful here, a terrible night last night, heaps
more snow. I am writing this letter after lunch, about 2 o'clock and up to
the present no letters for anyone, I understand from Miss Ashby that the
Mail Van is stuck in a snow drift at Chalk Hill I think she said, so perhaps
our letters will not arrive until quite late.

It was a topping letter I had from you yesterday my darling and
where you say the next time the 13th Feb comes round I shall be with
you even if I have to desert to come. I hope and trust I shall be with you
Frank, married to you I mean, next Feb is 12 long months from now
and I do not believe we shall be married even by then. I hate to think
of waiting so long. I would not mind one tiny scrap about you being
out there if we were only married, and after the War is over (and God
knows when that will be) we shall have to wait such a long time, you do
understand how I feel and what I mean do you not? It is because of my
great love for you my darling one, that makes the time of waiting seem
so long.

The letters are in, kid, and one from you, No. 21 this time. Quite a long
letter and a jolly nice one too.

I am so glad you have been honoured with one of the gilt wafers from
Bob, I remember her buying them when we were shopping in Bedford and
the great care she took of them bringing them home.

Yes, I do realise that I have asked you four, I say four separate times
about your cigarettes as to if I should send them out to you every week,
and why the Devil I want to know did you not reply straight away
when I first asked you instead of keeping me waiting about 14 months,
but I hold the reins in this deal and unless you are very careful and not
criticise my failing memory too much I shall send cigarettes and tobacco

<u>bought with your money</u> not to Salonica [sic] but to France to someone awfully nice I know out there.

Your dear sweetheart I do love you, your last letters have been topping. I am glad you are feeling a tiny bit happy, do my letters really cheer you up in the way you say they do?

Again thanking you for your great kindness to me, my dear husband goodbye.

Your very own, Nell

1 March 1916   Number 16

My own darling,

Twenty six weeks last Sunday since I saw you, six whole months. I wonder how much longer Frank dear, it just seems all one can do is to keep on wondering. Thanks my darling for your last letter, No. 23, which I received on Monday dear the 28th. I much enjoyed reading about your birthday dinner and the Menu I thought was great. Then you go on to say you went away to your own room (I mean tent) and stuck up my photograph and talked to me and then you say 'and when I turned in, dreamt of you and you were loving me quite a lot Nell and ____ ____ ____!, you dear sweetheart I wish I had been there, not when you woke up, I mean when you first turned in. Really, Frank dear, I do begin to think I shall have forgotten how to love you if you stay away from me very much longer, but I am not quite sure if I ever did know how to love you properly, tell me please, do you think I did?

I am glad you are effected [sic] the same way as myself re. your letter where you say, 'Kid dear I love you awfully just at this very minute' and you say 'please tell me you are glad'. Yes, my darling, I am glad, not only glad that you love me for tiny minutes but for always and always, don't you Frank, but I know exactly what you mean my husband, there are times when I too love you so much that I can hardly breathe. My God Frank how I love you, I wonder if you know how much.

I have sent into Luton today for your tobacco and cigarettes and I will post them to you tomorrow without fail. I could not send them before my darling, owing to the Luton roads being blocked with snow drifts, the

Carriers have not been able to go to Luton since Wednesday last week. The weather is now improving, the snow going, but very slowly.

No darling, you do not appear to have received my three letters posted to you Dec 7th, 11th and 12th. Tell me when you reply to this if you have received them because I did keep an outline of Dec 7th letter and if you like I will write it, or as much as I can remember of it, again to you.

All my other letters appear to have reached you but the idea of numbering them is just fine, as I said once before I cannot understand why we did not think of it sooner.

I am awfully glad you are fit; it is a relief to know you are quite well. I rather hope there will be a letter from you this afternoon, but there now I just want a letter from you every day, every post I believe, and then I should not be satisfied.

Goodbye my husband-to-be.

Always sweetheart,

Your very own, Nell

2 March 1916   Number 17

Dear old Frank,

I sent you a long letter yesterday so this one is going to be quite a short one, only as I promised yesterday in my letter to send your tobacco etc., today I am going to do so.

My darling, I was a tiny bit unhappy last night when I went to bed and after I was in bed I lay awake thinking about you for quite a long time.

I wonder how you are looking really Frank just now. Six months, I suppose it is possible for people to alter in appearance in that time. I do wish it were possible for you to send me a photograph of yourself, if only a snapshot, please don't think me quite mad darling but I do want one.

The last six months to me in some ways seems six years, and I am jolly sure I look at least six years older than when you last saw me, I wonder what your opinion will be supposing it is twelve months before we meet again, do you think you will be disappointed Frank, and perhaps wish you had not taken me nearly three years ago to the Leighton Buzzard Horse Show? Do you remember that night kid? When we went up into a sort of a tiny Drawing Room and we stayed on up there for a long time, and I made you admit to liking me a little bit and then coming home you said after all you thought you would like to stay on at Dunstable, that was if you could come over to Toddington.

You dear darling, I do not know why sweetheart but somehow I always look back upon this first night at Leighton Buzzard as just one of our own nights, do you understand what I mean by one of our nights? Please tell me dearest, although perhaps then I did not realise how things were going to turn out, but I do know that it was through this particular night that made the whole of Tommy's holiday seem less certain, made me feel that even with Tommy about the house I wanted you to be here as well.

Frank dear, there the thing remains. I met you quite a long time ago now and very soon found out that I wanted you, wanted you to love me, and you darling, how did you feel about it? I know how you felt. I need not ask. I had pretty plain proof at Christmas 1913 did I not? And you still love me and one day you will marry me and then I shall be your wife in name.

With all the love I am capable of,

Your very own, Nell
P.S. I am enclosing two Daily Mirror's. I thought I would like you to see the two sketches 'Salonika Circus' and not forgetting 'Miss Lloyd George'. Frank dear, judging by the sketch, how would you like to marry her?

7 March 1916　　Number 18

My own darling one,

I have not sent you a letter for four days dear and the last one I sent was enclosed with your Tobacco etc., last Thursday March 2nd and perhaps by the time this reaches you, you will not have received the parcel and you will be wondering what is the matter but Frank the last two letters received from you, Nos. 23 and 24, the first one was written on March the 14th and the second on the 18th so there was four days in between the two, you are not writing to me so often as you had used to do, why darling? Please tell me. The reason why I have not been able to write to you for a day or two, is, I have been rather busy in the house, also Bob has been home for her half term weekend, and when she is at home I do not know how it is but I seem to be always busy, what with her hair to be washed, and general repairs to her clothes and the remainder of the time both of us fussing round, the time seems to go quickly, she returned to school this morning on the 8.22 train. It was a terrible morning for her, we have had a lot more snow and it was snowing very hard this morning when she left home but of course naturally she thought it a huge joke.

Now about your last letter to me Frank darling, I was awfully glad to hear you had received the three December letters. I think you have been very lucky because sweetheart up to January 25th you have received all my letters and parcels, do you not agree with me Frank in saying you have been very lucky?

Thanks darling so much for your last letter. I liked it awfully, specially so where you say 'A boy – ours Nell, cuddled right up to you and I'll bet he will put his left hand on it just as you always wanted me to do'. Do you know kid I do not think I had remembered about it all the time you have been away and when I read your letter it all came back to me, of course sweetheart your left hand with the two rings I remember. Have you still got both the rings dear, or have you managed to loose [sic] them? I liked them so much on your dear finger. I do not think you would loose [sic] them, I think you would be very distressed if you did because I gave them to you 'Your wife but not in name'.

I love you my dearest one and have you no idea, not even now, as to when you will be home, April, May, June, July or when, tell me – I am just starving for you Frank and now that we are getting all this beastly snow and no one much coming in I am feeling very lonely.

I am so glad you liked my little curl. I thought you would when I saw him, I mean before I cut him off. I was delighted to hear even possessing that tiny bit of me made you feel less lonely, thank you my darling so much.

Please keep on loving me and write to me Frank more often than you have been doing just lately, because I want you to, and without your letters very often I could not go on, I should not try to.

Goodbye my own true darling, you are [my] Frank are you not? Please tell me.

Your wife-to-be, Nell

                                              10 March 1916   Number 19

Frank, my own darling,

Many thanks dear for your letter No. 25 received this morning.

I have been frightfully anxious all the week about not hearing from you, do you know I have only had two letters from you in a fortnight again. I have been thinking just lately that you can only be writing to me once a week, but I have compared the dates of your last two letters and I find No. 24 is dated Feb 18th and No. 25 Feb 20th so there is only two days in between which is not so bad, but Frank to have to wait a week for a letter is just too beastly. It is a jolly good job for you the dates of the two letters were in your favour, if not I should have given you a damned good slating.

Thanks, darling, for your kind inquiry re. my foot, I am pleased to say it has not bothered me quite so much as it did some time ago, in fact hardly at all now. It was quite nice of you to have remembered it, but could you forget after all the fuss I have made about it and the one night when I cried, do you remember? But I have suffered very severe pain from this particular foot several times, but I think perhaps it is rheumatic gout. Just lately I have been able to rest quite a lot and I am really feeling top hole.

You dear old sweetheart just for the moment I could not tell you the date for certain because darling ever since you have been away I have not bothered to remember, but there is one very sure thing about it, I always know with a vengeance when my day of reckoning is here, so when it rolls round again darling I will let you know without fail. Are you quite sure you will not mind if you do arrive back at an awkward time, I believe you would mind if you had to be sent back to Salonica [sic] without, and of course under certain circumstances I was going to say it would not be possible but if I remember rightly I found you always amorous and not over particular, tell me am I right? You know what I mean do you not my sweetheart? But it was always jolly nice, just lovely.

In your letter darling where you say 'I am selfish enough to be a tiny bit glad, anyhow it means there is no one worrying you, to put vulgarly, smelling around'. Frank dear perhaps you may not believe me but I am continually having to choke men off. There are crowds of soldiers and of course officers in Luton again now, the Northamptonshire Yeomanry are still there but the officer men are quite nice, three or four of them are over occasionally for tea, they are really decent fellows. I am quite sure you would think so if you met them.

By the way dear, before I forget, I had a letter from Tommy yesterday. There was nothing in it really of importance, he asks me to write to him. But I wanted you to know that I have heard from him. I do not want to keep anything away from you because I love you so much, and I do hope they will let you soon come home. I want to see you my own darling.

I was so sorry hear about your dose of rheumatism brought on by your tent collapsing and your clothes getting wet through, poor darling what an existence for you, Frank, out there, I trust my dearest one it is only a slight attack you are suffering from. I shall be anxious for your next letter. Goodbye my husband,
With all my love,

Always your very own, Nell

13 March 1916　　Number 20

Frank, my own darling,

The last letter I got from you was Friday last, March 10th and the letter before that one there was a full week in between, I am getting awfully fed up about not hearing from you oftener. Sweetheart in my last letter I promised to let you know the date, it has arrived sometime during the night, but we will say March 13th so count dear three clear days from now and then three weeks and you should not be more than a day or two out either way.

I was awfully poorly yesterday Frank, I did not feel well when I first got up, not really. I rested in the afternoon and then at 5 o'clock I went down into the kitchen to make a cup of cocoa and then the feeling was just too beastly for words. I was really frightened Frank, I quite thought I was going to faint, I laughed about it afterwards but then dear I was all alone in the house but I was quite alright in about 10 minutes and bustled about and made up the fires ready for the evening. During the night I found out how things were so I just thought 'Oh, this accounts for my little faint feeling of yesterday tea time'.

I thought of you my darling when I looked into the glass just to see, you know Frank, if I was really going to die because if you remember when I had used to get very tired you have many times remarked about my great big eyes and yesterday they were more or less like saucers. I was awfully glad I did think of you because it seemed to buck me up and made me feel better.

No news from the village. Today is Monday, on Wednesday I will post your Tobacco, etc.

Frank sweetheart on Feb 21st I posted you a letter, No. 13, no doubt by the time this letter reaches you, you will have replied to it, and told me all about what I asked you in it. It is no use, kid, you will have to keep on telling me you love me, I am finding the time now so awfully long since you went away, it will soon be seven months.

Tell me Frank that I am the very last woman that you loved. I do not mind, not the tiniest bit asking you this, you have never touched another woman for years, have you? only me, tell me my husband and I shall not be a fool for believing you, shall I?

I love you, as I feel sure it is not possible for another woman to love you, not quite in the same way. I have given myself body and soul to you so I can ask you all these things and if you do think I am a tiny bit unfair please forgive me, it is because of my great love for you that makes me feel troubled sometimes.

I do hope I get a letter tomorrow. Goodbye my darling.
With all my love,

Your wife-to-be, Nell

16 March 1916   Number 21

Frank, my own darling,

Just received your letter No. 26 dated 26.2.16 and your letter before this one No. 25 dated 20.2.16. I have worked out this little sum for you so that you will see it is six whole days, please don't forget but as you have apologised so nicely and said 'please forgive old girl', just this once I will but never again, and what I am going to tell you is this. One of the Northamptonshire Yeomanry Officers possesses a very nice car, a 60 H.P. Rolls Royce, and several times I have been asked to go out in it (although the man that owns it is only 25 years of age). So if ever there is another lapse of six whole days, well you will jolly well know what to expect.

I am frightfully sorry about the parcels darling, up to the present there are four to be acknowledged, this one today making five. I suppose you are wanting your Cigarettes etc. awfully badly.

Thanks my sweetheart, in your letter where you say 'Since I last saw you my wife I have seen thousands of women of all nationalities and classes but not a single one who interested me in the least', and you mean this Frank I know you do, there are times as I have told you before when I feel frightfully jealous and a tiny bit afraid that you may be tempted and not only tempted but go to see some woman. Perhaps in a way it is unfair of me, but no, a thousand times no, it is not unfair, you must never go. I wish I could tell you or write it down on paper, I mean just how I feel when I think and picture another woman in my place where you are concerned. In the same positions that I have been in, as you say in your letter, 'the touch of your living flesh and to feel your breath on my face and press close to your breast for a few minutes'.

Thank you my darling. Frank, it is all of these things that I think, all these things that I want, and knowing how you too must be feeling (you have been away from me nearly seven months) makes me feel sometimes a tiny bit afraid. Write to me sweetheart and tell me you quite understand what I mean, and how I feel, and that you will always keep straight for my sake. Really kid when I just think of another woman and you, my darling, my heart seems almost to cease beating and I am nearly suffocated.

I must not write any more today because I have your little parcel to
pack and sew up.

Goodbye my husband-to-be.

Always your very own, Nell

20 March 1916   Number 22

Frank darling,

I received both your letters this morning, No. 27 dated 29.2.16 and No. 28
dated 3.3.16. No. 27 is the registered letter containing [a] cheque for £15.
I do not know quite what I am going to say to you in this letter, or how
I am going to explain, but first of all please let me tell you that you have
hurt my feelings very much in writing to me, Frank, in the way that
you have done, and I do think you might have taken into consideration
that our letters had crossed, and then when my letter No. 11 was sent to
you asking for a cheque I had not received any money from you since
December until February 25th, even then I only expected a cheque for £10
as by your own suggestion that was the amount you promised, which was
very very kind of you Frank dear, and all I expected.

I did think yesterday morning when I first read your letter that never
as long as I lived would I ask you for money again, but of course I shall,
if not before then after we are married, I should have to. I am sorry
there has been this misunderstanding, kid, and particularly so that it
should have come about over money matters. I suppose in a way it serves
me right, I should have got out of the house and by so doing have been
independent or at least much more so than I am now.

I feel sure dear when you get this letter you will feel sorry that you
have been unkind to me. I am frightfully sensitive Frank about this
money business because I do know, darling, I have no right to expect it
from you.

Anyhow, yesterday you succeeded in making me very unhappy, just
sick to death of life generally. I managed to keep back the tears until after
breakfast and then I made up for lost time. I thought during the evening
that it would never be 10 o'clock so that I could be alone and just think,

and even when the time came, I was too jolly miserable to do anything else besides sit and cry. Frank, is it possible that even now we do not understand each other?

Referring to your letter you say, 'Further, what do you mean by saying that the whole thing is not very satisfactory'. Good God, don't you understand? Do you yourself think the whole thing satisfactory? I should be a fool in trying to explain. I am just going on living as I have done now for 2½ years, loving you passionately, every tiny bit of you I want, and at the same time going to bed night after night knowing that I am married to a man whom I loathe and then you say 'what do I mean by saying the whole thing is not satisfactory'.

I note what you say as to writing to me, and you go on to say 'neither have I a Whisky and Soda or something at my elbow to stimulate my thoughts'. I am glad because as I have thought for a long time now that if you never touch whisky and soda or any other stimulant again, you, no doubt like me, have had your share.

I am not going to write any more today, perhaps when you have read this you will understand the particular mood I am in and at the same time feel sorry for me.

But I can't finish this letter until I have thanked you for your last cheque of £15. Thank you very much Frank dear, and I will perhaps write you again in a day or two.

I love you, as you know I do, but Frank, well I don't know, there are some things I cannot understand, but I do understand that I love you as no other woman will ever love you. I would willingly give my life for you, although you are unfair to me. Frank dear, you have been unfair to me a lot times have you not?
Your very own Nell

28 March 1916   Number 26

Frank, my own darling,

In reply to this letter please tell me which of my letters you have not received, I mean dear those of mine that are numbered because, Frank, in your letters I got yesterday, Nos. 32, 33 and 34, you were rather mixed up. In your letter No. 32 you acknowledge my 13 and 14 then in your next letter which was written four days later you wonder what has happened to my number 13 letter. The two letters you received from me on March 4th were both numbered 15. I am sorry but I feel sure they should have been Nos 15 and 16.

I was awfully pleased at getting three letters from you yesterday. I did not receive them until about 7 o'clock, I went up to town yesterday specially to order a coat and skirt which although ordered, I believe I shall hate when finished. You see dear the fashions have changed such a lot during the last six months, full skirts very short are now being worn and the coats are ridiculous, short little things full all round the waist, but at the same time I have not ordered one of these coats and I think I have taken great care in ordering so that my coat is not too extreme.

I returned home on the 5.40 out from St Pancras, it was really quite a nice day. I much enjoyed being away from home. Last evening coming up from Harlington station it commenced to snow and during the latter part of the evening and through the night we had a lot of snow, about 15 inches in depth, and now all this morning torrents of rain and very foggy, this afternoon, now, as I sit writing more snow, lots of it falling down and a terrific wind. I never remember anything like the weather we have had for the last six weeks. I am getting very tired of the long dreary Winter.

I do not know which of your three letters I like the best, they are all topping, thank you for all of them Frank dear, and thank you so much for what you have told me in them and where you say 'I can give you my word of honour that I have kept absolutely straight in thought and deed since the minute I said goodbye to you; not only since then either my wife but since the day I first met you.' Again, thank you Frank and I believe you, you have made me happy my darling by just writing to me all about it.

I do not remember anything at all about the small photograph that you say was torn from one of the Mirrors, do you think I took it out kid? If so, it would have been cut out (not torn) most carefully but perhaps, dear, someone else removed it.

No, I do not think there is any sign of you winning your bet re. Mrs Fletcher. I think if at all possible she will have to be remade, I do not know whatever you will do, but I am thinking it will be a case of pay out for

you Frank. I wrote to you last Sunday dear and enclosed the letter with
your Tobacco and Cigarettes and upon thinking about [it] I feel sure
I did not number this letter, it should of course be No. 25, and I posted
the parcel quite early yesterday morning, about 8.20, before I went to the
station to catch the 9.26.

Please tell me if there is anything else you want sent out, as I have said
before do not be afraid to ask me. Have you finished your Chelsea Bank
envelopes, if so, shall I send some more? And how about Café au Lait,
shall I send some on to you? I do not send you anything off my own bat,
not really, because I would so much rather you say what you want, so
please do my own sweetheart, just anything I will send out to you.
Goodbye my darling husband,

Always your very own, Nell

1 April 1916   Number 27

Frank, my own darling,

In my last letter to you sweetheart I spoke about the dreadful weather we
were having and after I had finished writing to you which was Tuesday
last, letter No. 26, the storm increased in violence. Frank dear it was really
terrible, snow and wind – even the oldest inhabitants of Toddington
cannot remember anything like it. There are about 20 trees down on the
Manor Estate, but the trees are down everywhere. The roads are still
blocked with fallen timber and snow. Darling, I think owing to the storm
we do not seem to have received any letters or hardly at all since Tuesday,
and then last night the confounded Zeppelins were over, trains held up, etc.
etc. It is 12 o'clock now and no post in yet. I am just wondering when I shall
receive the photographs. I have not heard from you since last Monday, I do
hope I shall soon hear, Frank, and I do want to get the photographs.

Do you really mean, sweetheart, that you still think at the end of the
Summer the show will be over? I cannot think so, Frank, but I do not
understand. I hope with all my heart darling you are right.

I am not feeling very bright today, not really, I just feel as if I must go
right away from here, at least for a week. I am waiting to hear what you

have to say about coming home and then kid, if you do not seem at all
sure about it, I think I shall try to get away for a day or two soon. I am
awfully fed up (I hate the expression fed up, but at the same time I think
it expresses one's feelings) with being here, particularly so during the
last fortnight, but one cannot wonder at it, can they Frank? I am jolly
sure I do not grumble without a cause. I do sometimes think of what Mrs
Bonner always says, that I shall never be able to live, or settle down, in a
private house. Of course she is wrong in that, and she does not know how
much I really love you and as I am going to live with you in a private
house [it] will make all the difference in the world as to my settling down.
You will always be good to me Frank, and always remember that I hate
monotony and please promise never to leave me too much alone.

Sunday, 2 April 1916

I did not have time to finish this letter to you yesterday sweetheart, and
Frank dear the post came in but there was no letter from you, and again
today no letter, it is a week tomorrow since I last heard from you, a whole
week kid.

Thank God I have managed to get through one more Saturday night.
I have just read your No. 33 letter again, it is a topping letter, Frank,
I love it – you say darling 'I know how beastly everything is for you my
sweetheart and I want you to believe that I really do feel for you', and you
go on to say 'The one fact that we both know exactly what we want is the
salvation of us both' and you ask me if I agree with you. Yes, I do agree
with you my darling. I often wonder what I should have done during the
last two years if I had not met you, not only met you sweetheart but love
you in the way I do, but if I had never met you perhaps I should never
have found out how very little I cared for Bertie, but as things are I am
perfectly satisfied. I love you as I have never loved anyone else or ever
likely to, I just I just love you and want you, my husband, and from day
to day I live on the one thought that soon, as soon as possible, you will
make me your wife, as you say Frank, in name, thank you so much you
dearest of all men.

Goodbye my darling, I will not keep you quite so long for my next letter.

Your wife-to-be, Nell

P.S. I notice that I have written 'I just' twice. I dare not scratch it out or
you will wonder what it was I had wrote there. Nell

5 April 1916   Number 29

My own dearest sweetheart,

I do not remember what the back of the Magazine was like so it is an impossibility for me to feel jealous (as if I should) if you have still got it when this letter reaches you send it back to me, I should so like to see it. I got two letters from you yesterday Nos. 35 and 36, thanks dear so much, I was awfully pleased to get them as I had not heard from you for over a week.

Dear old Frank and you really do think this time that you are coming back to France. Of course I am frightfully pleased about it, but honestly darling I do not mind where you are as long as you are safe so that in the long run you will be quite fit and sound, dear, so we can be married very soon after. Frank darling you do know that I have always said no matter how badly hurt you get out there or how badly crippled, it would not make the slightest difference to me, if possible I should love you more than ever, but I worship you now Frank and I could not do more than that could I? But I would be so kind to you and so proud of you.

There are a number of talkative people who say that they think I am making a great mistake in not sticking to Armstrong and that by not doing so I am making the greatest mistake in my life, a mistake I shall live to regret, so perhaps my darling if it is your luck to get badly crippled in the War I shall then be able to prove to them that my whole life is yours and that if I am making a mistake in leaving Armstrong as they say, then I am perfectly willing to chance my luck. How I hate them all, Frank, but is it not an astonishing thing, kid, how so many people stick up for him, and how they seem to hate the idea of Bertie and I drifting apart, but at the same time Bertie seems to come in for all their pity, I am not considered. Thank God I am independent, I do not want their pity, neither do I want to know them. Every day I live more and more in a world of my own. I just want to go right away from everyone I know, to start absolutely a new life with you Frank, and if ever this is my luck, which I pray God it will be, I will take great care never to get to know a lot of people and I believe I have said before that if I have my kiddie then I should be perfectly happy, and outside people would not interest me one tiny bit. I went down to Bedford [...]

6 April 1916

My darling, I could not go on with this letter yesterday, I got so far and then a nasty crowd arrived from The George Hotel, Luton, but I will tell you about them in my next letter, so from where I left off. I went down to Bedford on Monday specially to see about your boots and to buy myself a hat and really survived the ordeal very well.

Sweetheart, I shall be sending your boots in a day or two because I have chosen a pair from stock size 7. If you remember Frank the pair you were wearing when soldiering in England you bought from stock did you not? The H make I mean. The pair of boots that I have chosen are made from quite heavy polishing leather, of course I gave them instructions as to nails and spur blocks, the assistant man at 'Kent & Costicks' (this is the shop in the High St) said he felt sure they would be suitable. I am a tiny bit uncertain as to the thickness of the soles but I thought if when you came home you did not think them quite thick enough they could go back to the shop to be made heavier. This the man said would be quite easy to do. So immediately I get them from Bedford I will post them on to you at once, I shall be really awfully anxious to hear what you have to say about them.

Sweetheart mine, how about the photographs? I am just dying to get them. I feel sure there will be one of yourself, I shall be most awfully disappointed if there is not, I love you my own darling and if it is only a tiny snapshot of your dear self it will be a great comfort to me. Goodbye my husband-to-be,

Your very own, Nell

7 April 1916   Number 29

Frank, my own sweetheart,

I explained to you yesterday in my letter all that I thought necessary about your boots dear and as they arrived yesterday on the second post I thought I would get them off today with your tobacco and cigarettes, also shampoo powders. I hope you will find the powders quite alright kid, the girl at Stavinski strongly recommended them. I should suggest, Frank, that you use half a powder to half a pint of very warm water as I feel sure, this quantity, you would find more than sufficient.

The girl also said there was no smell of Eucalyptus when the powder was dissolved, so I hope you will find them to your liking, please let me know my darling.

I am not feeling very well today, what with the time of the month, and a shocking cold I feel all to pieces. I believe I did tell you that things would be happening again on or about April 7th, well it was yesterday dear the 6th so I was not very far out was I sweetheart? So three clear days brings it to the 9th and three weeks from the next day so the next time darling on or about the 1st of May.

You asked me to tell you this and I love doing so because you want me to.

I have been very lucky this Winter in avoiding a cold, this is the first bad one since last August and I think almost as severe as the cold I had then, but I certainly hope it is not going to last quite as long as that one did, but I always think a bad cold makes one feel very beastly for the time being.

Still no news in the village darling, but referring to your letter No. 35, yes dear, several of the men who were attested under the Derby Scheme have been called up but of course Anderson, Lines and Tom Camp have been exempted – they are what I believe is called starred men, but I really do not understand it, at the same time I think as a great many more people think (at least now) that the Derby Scheme has been a farce from start to finish.

Thank you so much sweetheart for explaining to me about things, I was awfully interested when reading your letter. I am so glad you have explained, as one can gain so little by the papers.

Goodbye my darling, I love you so much my husband-to-be are you not?

Always your very own, Nell

14 April 1916　　Number 30

Frank, my own darling,

I feel sure you will be getting anxious about not hearing from me because the last time I wrote to you was a week today and the letter No. 29, sweetheart, was enclosed with your boots which of course by the time this reaches you, you may not have received because as you say the parcels seem to take a very long time to reach you. I have not felt the tiniest bit like writing during the last week, I do not know why, Frank. The kid is home for Easter and we have been busy at needlework.

I received a letter from you this morning, No. 42, but really sweetheart your letters do arrive in most peculiar order, a week today, no I mean a week tomorrow I received Nos. 38 and 39 then as I have just said this morning No. 42, so 40 and 41 are still to arrive. About your letters, kid, let me tell you. I have received them all up to number 36 with the one exception <u>No. 12</u>. I want to know what you said in this letter, why have I not received it? You are quite sure my darling you did send it, I mean, kid, was this number omitted, did you number one letter 11 and the next one 13 in mistake? Up to the present I have not received your recent letter No. 37, but of course I may do yet, I hope I shall.

I am sorry my dearest one about not writing to you for six whole days, please forgive me Frank dear, I will try to make up for lost time next week.

Do you know dear when I do let three or four days go past without writing to you I think of you such a lot, and keep of [sic] fidgeting about it and many times (and many times) I just think to myself I must write to Frank today, I really must.
(I dare not erase and <u>many times</u>)

Your No. 38 letter containing your description of the Air Raid, thank you so much darling, but at the same time it made me feel frightfully miserable and afraid for you. How very dreadful the whole thing is, you might have been killed. I often wonder what I should do if you do not live to come back to me, do you ever think about it my husband? I do very often, and I just wonder sometimes if you have really fixed up with somebody about letting me know the worst at once if you do get smashed up, we did once before, a long time ago, speak about this but I should like to know if you have made any arrangement as to this.

You quite understand do you not my darling? And forgive me for
being despondent but just at times kid I cannot help it. I love you
so passionately, you are my life, everything that is dear to me. I say
everything that is dear to me, I mean it my husband, as you know I love
Bob but in a different way my darling to the way in which I love you. You
are my all, without you I do not want to live.
I will write you again very soon.

Your wife Nell
P.S. When are you coming home? I love you and want you so badly,
Frank dear!

                                        17 April 1916   Number 31
Frank, my dearest one,

Your letter No. 37 arrived this morning for which many thanks. I was
awfully pleased to get it Frank dear, it is a nice letter and you have
explained to me about Tommy. I have thought about one or two of
his letters that have arrived from him recently and I did so hope that
when I heard from you, you would speak about the letter of Tommy's
that I had told you about, and in your letter that I got this morning
you have done so and you say 'Please don't be angry with me or think
me a cad but I don't want you to start writing to him regularly'. You
are quite right Frank my darling, it would no doubt be a most foolish
thing to do and I will not do so, and as you say, leave things as they
are until you get home. I love this letter No. 37 of yours and you say
'We love each other in a way that no one else can ever understand.'
It is so Frank is it not? I often think about the way I love you, it is
beyond all explanation, even if I wished I could not tell anyone. My
dear husband my love for you is to me a thing apart, just something
all by itself.
    You finish up your letter by saying 'God grant I may be able to make
you as happy as I shall be when I hold you in my arms'. I shall be happy
Frank, just too happy to speak. I shall want you to hold me as you have
done many times before but this time it will be different, after all these

long months without you, can you imagine what it will be like my husband, and then after, just to cuddle right down still in your arms and to sleep, and when I wake to feel you near me. Through the night, dear, to kiss you quite a lot of times, I know I shall. Sometimes I think it will be worth waiting for, but I hate being without you now.

I have no news for you kid, the village I think is more impossible than ever. You said in your letter that everything points to you getting home in May, about the end you say, I wonder Frank, I do hope you do but I am not going to think too much about it because perhaps after all you may not come. I have so many things I want to ask you about, your advice to me sweetheart means so much.

I am going to Bedford tomorrow, at least Bob and I are going, so Wednesday my darling I will post your tobacco etc. and no doubt write you again.

I do not think I will write any more today, I am just feeling a tiny bit miserable. I love you with all my heart Frank but just at times I miss you so much that I cannot help feeling miserable and you understand me kid do you not?

Goodbye my own true darling, I love you and trust you implicitly.

From your wife-to-be, Nell

19 April 1916   Number 32

Frank, my own darling,

I must not write a very long letter today dear, only I do so want to send your tobacco and cigarettes. Poor kid, and were you really reduced to smoking 'Woodbines'? I laughed over your No. 40 letter, it was topping particularly so where you refer to the Woodbines and say 'I have not yet got to the state of carrying a bit of one behind my ear but probably that will follow in due course'. Then you go on to tell me about your puppy who rejoices in the name of 'Shrapnel'. I was awfully interested, I should so love to see him, please tell me more about him when you reply to this.

Frank, sweetheart, of course in this letter No. 40 was your cheque for £15, it sounds all wrong just to say thank you for all your kindness to me in the way of money, you are indeed good to me but as you know darling

I could not live on here without your help but apart from that I do appreciate your kindness.

Since you have been away, or rather since last September, I believe it was Oct 10th when I received your first cheque of £10 and since then I have received £80 making £90 in all, but of course darling it is you that is keeping the home together. There is absolutely nothing doing in the house, days and days the takings do not exceed half a crown each day. I do not know if you will be surprised when I tell you that out of all the money I have had from you I have not been able to save a halfpenny, but I don't think we thought I should be able to save, did we? If I could manage to live on here was the idea was it not? Tell me Frank, I feel sometimes uncertain and bothered about it.

My darling I am quite sure I am not extravagant in any way, but the kid is a dreadful expense. We went to Bedford. I told you in my letter I posted to you Monday that Bob and I were going and with buying just the bare necessities for her I spent quite a lot of money. My darling when you come home we can talk it over, but I am more than thankful for your help and you believe me do you not Frank?

Sweetheart, you must forgive all mistakes in my letters particularly this one, I have had to leave it so many times. Pickering from Hockliffe has just been in and kept me talking for several minutes. Immediately he got into the place he said, 'how is Mr Armstrong and how is Captain Smith?' I replied saying I believed you were both quite well, I told him I had a letter from you yesterday but I had not heard from Bertie since long before Christmas, really Frank I have never seen a man look more surprised than he did, but he said nothing.
Goodbye my own true darling, I love you.

Your wife-to-be, Nell

21 April 1916   Number 33

My own dearest sweetheart,

Good Friday today and I just feel as if I must write to you. I wonder what we shall be doing this time next year, I wish I knew. My darling I am most awfully behind this week with my work but I don't care, I am going to write to you. Thank you dearest for your last two letters – Nos. 42 and 43. Number 43 arrived this morning for which many thanks.

Frank dear, before this letter reaches you, you will have received numbers of letters from me since my No. 22 letter and you will have found out long ago that you are forgiven, of course you are, because I love you so much.

I was awfully glad to hear from you this morning, and how strange you should have mentioned about the night we went to see 'Mr Will' because I too have thought about it quite a lot of late and only one day this week I was talking to Bob about it. I loved the whole evening of this particular day. I was very happy. I can see you as if it was only yesterday as you sat in the box at the Theatre, several times during the performance I just looked at you and loved you awfully.

I think the weather is a tiny bit better here just lately but still very unsettled, although today is very very nice, it is a perfect day really. I do so wish you were here so that we could go out. It is indeed comforting to read what you have to say about the War and I am quite sure you must long for the end. Yes, Frank dear, I can realise what it will mean to you and I think to a certain extent I can grasp what the strain of being out there is really like and what perhaps it will mean to you in years to come. I posted your Tobacco and Cigarettes on Wednesday, kid, the 19th, but I suppose you will get this letter before you receive the parcel.

I hate this paper, it is perfectly ghastly to write on. I have a pretty shrewd idea as to what it might be used for but even for that purpose it would be hopeless.

Up to the present dearest one I have received all your letters up to No. 43, with as I told you before the one exception, No. 12, and I have asked you in a previous letter to tell me about this missing one so do doubt by now darling you have explained it to me.

Frank, before I forget, I posted to you a letter dated Feb 14th, No. 10, I do not think you have received this letter because in it I asked you about sending matches out to you. You will have noticed that in your last several parcels I have not enclosed matches, as one is not supposed to send them, at least not to Salonica [sic] but I said in my letter if you very much wish it, I could send them and of course not declare them on the calico wrapping, but is it worth it? Tell me darling what I am to do please.

I must really finish up now my dear husband-to-be, please keep on loving me because I want you to so much.

Goodbye my darling, take great care of yourself, I love you dearest of all men.

Your very own, Nell

26 April 1916   Number 34

My own dearest one,

I really do begin to wonder if I shall have time to write to you as often as I have done, I mean, dear, now that the weather is so much better I am sure to be busy in the house and Frank dear, being single handed, I hardly know how I shall manage. Easter Monday all but killed me. I never remember feeling so tired as I did that night when I went to bed.

But no doubt I shall get through, I shall have to somehow. I have very firmly made up my mind not to engage anyone in Mrs Bonner's place, I would not do so under any circumstances whatever because I should just feel if I did, that it meant staying on here and you know jolly well I have no intention of doing so. But I shall write to you my darling just whenever I get the tiniest opportunity.

Bob returns to school on Monday next, then perhaps I shall have rather more time, really, kid, the last three weeks have been too dreadful, what with the care of the house, trying to arrange about Bob's clothes and a hundred and one other small things not worth mentioning, I have been bothered almost beyond endurance, but just at these times sweetheart I think it is no use getting worried because it can't be for very much longer, I must just stick to it for the time being, and then I go on to think of all the lovely times we are going to have later on when I am married to you and after a bit you know kid I feel better and life seems brighter.

I got two of your letters this morning, Nos. 44 and 45. I was awfully pleased but Frank you say, 'Even if I cannot get home to you for a few more months you will still be waiting and wanting me'. Yes I shall still be waiting and wanting you my sweetheart, but a few more months you say kid, it is too bad. In a letter I had from you a day or two ago you said you might be home about the end of May, but at the same time I did not believe you. I do not for a tiny moment think you will come home from Salonica [sic] until the war is over. Of course dear if you get back to France I might then see you home. Just sometimes sweetheart I want to see you so badly that I hardly know what to do and then at other times I feel I do not mind about you being right away out in Salonica [sic] if you are only safe.

I was sorry to read that you were feeling dicky after the injection of anti-cholera germs, poor old Frank, but I suppose it was really necessary to have this done.

I have just read your No. 44 letter again, it is a topping letter my darling, I love it. Such excitement just now, Frank dear, a balloon over Toddington which appeared to be coming down, so I said to Bob come along kid let us go, so off we started then we saw Ruffett tearing off on his old motor bike with side car so we shouted please give us a ride (do not forget that I had not explained to Rose we were going out). He pulled up and we packed in, right away down the Tingrith lane we went, and then we ran over three huge fields and got there just as they were rolling up the canvas, quite a number of people had arrived from the village before we got there. Six naval men were with the balloon, one or two of them quite nice looking boys, please do not be jealous. Anyway, Bob and I thoroughly enjoyed our little pleasure trip, particularly the ploughed field. I left this letter of yours half finished but had the presence of mind to lock the C. Room door and take the key with me.

For today my darling I must finish. Goodbye my husband-to-be, I love you.

Always your very own, Nell

29 April 1916   Number 35

Frank, my own dearest one,

I am so jolly poorly today, kid. I have come downstairs specially to write to you but I am feeling better than I did first thing this morning, nothing really serious Frank, I think nerves chiefly and perhaps I did rather too much at Easter but you know how strong I am really do you not? So surely three days hard work should not have knocked me up, then again the time of the month is nearly here and you understand.

I am writing you today dear because I want to do so, and because I am a tiny bit afraid if I do not write today I may not be able to until Tuesday. Tomorrow Sunday I have Bob's packing to do and then Monday I take her back to school.

By the time this letter reaches you, you will have heard the news about Ireland, during the last two or three days I have been inundated with inquiries for Mr Armstrong so you can quite well imagine how I have been feeling. I hate it, I particularly detest to hear his name mentioned in any one way whatever. Some people I answer fairly politely, others I am damned rude to and I am glad of it. I could annihilate some of them Frank, and I think let them wait, and when they know we are married will it not be a delightful smack in the face for them.

I seem to have had so little time with the kid this holiday, but you see dear she only had three weeks and then there was Easter which took up quite a lot of my time. We have both very firmly come to the conclusion that we would much rather live in a private house with you my darling. I told Bob she must wait until she was asked, she replied saying she considered she was already your sweetheart, I told her I did not care what she thought but I was going to keep house for you, she was delighted and several times she has said since (when she was cuddled right up near to me) 'Mama did you really mean it?'

I have not heard from you since I last wrote to you, which was Wednesday last, but I may do tomorrow, I hope so. Frank my darling do you think you will be able to pay your account at Harry Hills before it is again sent in, please tell me.

April 29th, eight months today since I last saw you, and I love you just the same my husband as I did then, as I shall always love you. Goodbye my own true sweetheart until Tuesday when I will write to you again.

Your very own, Nell

2 May 1916   Number 36

Frank, my own darling,

Yes, I did send you tobacco and cigarettes in between the 2nd of March and the 26th, it was on the 16th (No. 21 letter enclosed). I posted you the usual quantity, namely 30 Richmond Gem, 2oz Three Nuns and about ½ a box of Gold Flake in packets. I may have enclosed papers but I am not quite sure. So this is two parcels missing now, No. 12 letter enclosed with parcel posted Feb 18th and this one. What a nuisance it is Frank, I am sorry darling.

The next parcel is the one with your boots posted on April 8th. I do hope nothing will happen to this one. I really believe I forgot to tell you when I wrote to you about the boots that the leather they were made from is quite the heaviest procurable in a polishing leather, I mean dear that if Kent & Costicks had made them specially for you, they would have been from this same thickness of leather but of course as I explained to you before, the soles could have been heavier so, Frank darling, when you again ask me to order boots for you please tell me the exact thickness of sole you require.

I received two letters from you this morning sweetheart, Nos. 47 and 48. I was awfully pleased, today is Tuesday and I had not heard from you since last Wednesday, a week all but a day.

In my last letter to you, which was Saturday, I was awfully poorly and then Sunday things happened and yesterday I had to take the kid back to school so by the time I got back home last evening I felt rather weary, just lately I have been suffering from most frightful neuralgia, I think perhaps it is because I am a tiny bit run down. I worry so much sometimes Frank dear, you know I do, I can't help doing so, but I think I shall take your advice and go away for a day or two. Frank sweetheart you don't want me to go a tiny bit, not really. Your letter amuses me where you say 'Tell me sweetheart where you will go to and please my darling don't look too nice while you are away'.

You dear stupid old thing, of course I should try to look just as nice as possible, I wonder if I could get myself off if I tried very hard, but I do not think I shall go away, I should hate to be away from here without you, but anyway Frank if I do decide I will without fail let you know. In a letter I sent you dated April 7th, No. 29, I told you I should be (not feeling very well thank you) on or about May 1st. I was a day out again, it happened quite early Sunday morning, April 31st, so three days counting April 31st as one, and then three weeks from May 3rd, brings it to, on or about May 24th. Do you want me to still keep on telling you this, Frank dear, tell me please.

I am so anxious to receive the photographs, and thank you so much where you say you hope to send them along with one or two of yourself quite soon, I shall love them.

Thank you for sending a list of my letters as you have received them so there is three missing. I wonder if either of them will turn up eventually. I suppose the parcel posted Feb 18th with letter No. 12 enclosed has gone to the bottom, but you must let me know about the more recent parcel of March 16th, this of course you may get, I hope so. I am awfully afraid you find my letters very uninteresting regarding the news of the village but honestly Frank I tell you all there is to be told. Constable Emery is leaving Toddington tomorrow, he is going to Leighton Buzzard and I understand that Sgt Dennis is to manage with the assistance of the Special Constables until the war is over. I think Emery would have gone a long time ago, only the powers that be could not find a house sufficiently large for his thirteen children.

I must not write any more today my darling. Thursday I will post your Tobacco and Cigarettes.

All my love dearest, goodbye until I write again.

Your wife-to-be, Nell

4 May 1916   Number 37

My own dearest sweetheart,

Thanks so much dear for your No. 46 letter received yesterday morning, Wednesday, I was awfully glad it came because I was feeling undecided about going to Town to fit my coat and skirt, so after reading your letter I found there was several things you wanted and I thought it could all be done under the same journey so I went up on the 11.51 from Harlington and returned on the 5.40 out from St Pancras.

I wonder what you will say when you first look at your new pipe, Frank dear, I was awfully nervy about buying it, but even when I read your letter upstairs I felt sure there was not a pipe of yours about the house with the exception of a very old one with a broken mouthpiece, but I have had a new mouthpiece fitted to this pipe and will send it to you next week, I am not sending both today dear in case the parcel gets lost. I feel sure Frank that several of your pipes were left at Dunstable, either at The Sugar Loaf or more likely at the office. I remember quite well you making inquiries from here soon after you went to Tunbridge Wells and taking away the one or two old ones that were about. Anyway, kid, I have done my best in choosing your new pipe and if you are not quite satisfied, well just say 'What do women know about pipes'. Of course I do know from experience how fussy men are. I will send the remainder of your things next week, your Café au Lait, etc.

I am sending you a sketch of a coat that I felt awfully inclined to have copied for mine (I don't think) but I thought it would give you too much of a shock if I was wearing it when meeting you on your return home. Really kid I cannot describe my coat to you but perhaps I will ask Fishers to outline the thing on paper and I will send the sketch on to you, the skirt is fairly short, I think I shall like it.

Frank my darling I had a letter from Tommy this morning. I would send it on to you only there is really nothing in it. You will be sorry to hear he is in the hospital suffering he says from a ruptured adhesion, he goes on to explain that it is something to do with his last operation and has evidently been brought on again through strain of riding or something of the sort. I feel frightfully sorry for him, really Frank he has had rough luck as regards his health for such a long time now. I shall reply to this letter of Tommy's, perhaps one day next week, and my darling you know I will be very careful in the way I word my letter.

Sometimes I think I ought not to write to him, but I don't think it matters, do you my husband, you do not mind, not really do you? Please tell me.

Thank you so much for your message to the kid where you say 'Give her my love and tell her not to grow too big'. I did not receive this letter until Wednesday and she returned to school Monday so I could not give her your message. There is no two ways about her growing big, she is certainly doing that but I think only well proportioned sweetheart, not too big. We had quite a lot of fun together and several times both of us laughed and kept on laughing until we cried all about nothing.

Are you still feeling quite well Frank? I hope you are for my sake dearest. I want you to keep awfully well because I am quite sure after we are married I shall want quite a lot of patching up. I have felt beastly this last week, I did say this morning I would go over to Dr Waugh's this evening for some medicine, but I do not know if I shall change my mind. Perhaps now things are over again I shall feel better, but it is nothing really to worry about I am quite sure Frank. I think it is through lack of attention so please hurry up and come home and do those things that you have left undone for at least eight months.

I love you my dearest one and want you, you know I do.

Always your very own, Nell

8 May 1916   Number 38

Frank, my own darling,

The enclosed telegram explains itself, it arrived here Saturday afternoon at about 2 o'clock although handed in I notice the day before which was Friday. I have not replied to the telegram and neither have I heard further or seen anything of him, but at the same time I have expected him to walk in every minute since the confounded wire arrived. I am awfully unhappy again Frank, although I always think you never understand as to why I should be.

I wish to God he would come to a definite understanding, I am so tired of being disturbed, so tired of living this make believe sort of life. I am frightfully miserable and down in the mouth today, more so today than yesterday and yet there is nothing I can do, please try to understand how I am feeling Frank. I love you so much, if I did not the whole thing would be so easy, I should have got out of this house long ago and gone up to Town to live, and if I could not have earned sufficient money honestly then the remainder I should had to have borrowed, but that is neither here nor there kid, I do love you, and the only thing for me to do is to try and put up with things, at least until you come home. Sometimes I wonder Frank, only suppose this War goes on for another two years, of course I know dear you say that you feel convinced it will be over by the end of the Summer but only suppose it goes on and on indefinitely, tell me what have I to do, have I to still stay on here? Surely you have thought about it, please tell me in your reply to this, I mean dear, will you wish me to stay on under the same circumstances as now but even if it is your wish I shall not be able to do so.

Please forgive me my darling for writing to you like this, and as I have said before try to understand, but I just feel you have been away from me so long, nearly eight and a half months now and I miss you my husband, what a difference in my life it has made but I am glad, a thousand times glad, I would not have it otherwise and if I was only married to you I should not mind nearly so much about you being right away from me for so long.

Goodbye Frank dearest, I will write you again quite soon, if of course he stays away, please God he will.

Your very own, Nell

15 May 1916　Number 39

Frank, my own dearest one,

I believe I am feeling a tiny bit mean in not having written to you for quite a number of days, nearly a week Frank. I am sorry kid, please forgive me but in the meantime I have sent you papers so that proves you have not been forgotten. Darling when your two letters arrived this morning, Nos. 52 and 54 (two topping letters sweetheart and a cheque for £15) I did feel frightfully sorry about the lapse of seven days between my letters. I have not felt the tiniest bit like writing, day after day I have just felt as if I couldn't touch a pen, and neither have I. You see, Frank darling, in the first instance I had Bertie's wire and that disturbed me frightfully, he has not been home and I have not heard from him but after the wire I could not settle down, at least not for a day or two. I am feeling better again now and I will write to you very very often to make up for lost time.

You dear sweetheart, I love your letters received this morning. You did love me a tiny bit extra when you wrote them, I feel sure you did, and where you say that I gave myself to you absolutely knowing that I was getting into trouble but not caring (you quoted this, dear, from a previous letter of mine and I mean it a thousand times my husband). Frank dear, how I have loved you, love you now and how I shall love you again when you come home. Sometimes, when I am thinking about the perfect times we have had together I wonder how many men and women under the same circumstances have felt as we have done, very few ay Frank? The first nights we spent in London, were they not lovely nights darling? I think of those nights so many times, even after I had loved you when we had cuddled down really for sleep your arms had to be all over me, I had to feel you quite close, and through the night when either of us wakened it was Nell darling or Frank darling, do you remember? You are quite right sweetheart it is utterly impossible for me, too, to try and explain on paper how much I love you. I worship you until nothing else in the whole world seems to matter.

I have no news for you from the village. I cannot think of the tiniest little scrap of news.

I had a letter yesterday from Connie Burton, for the moment I forget if I told you she is married and living on at home with her father. She asked very kindly after you in her letter.

I was awfully amused the other night kid, Mrs Bonner and Miss Potts were chatting to me in the C. Room, you remember dear I had not been very well and they were asking me if I felt better. Mrs Bonner thinks I am getting so very thin, I told them I was feeling much better, I then turned round to Mrs Bonner and said I thought I must be pregnant, she said 'Good Heavens, has it been sent over in a letter then?' Is she not a saucy old thing, Frank?

Goodbye my husband-to-be, I love you and want you just awfully badly. I have not thanked you for your cheque have I but I am going to do so now, thank you very much Frank dear, you are more than kind to me. Take great care of yourself sweetheart mine.

Always your very own, Nell

17 May 1916   Number 40

Frank, my dearest one,

Enclosed please find darling your Tobacco, Cigarettes, Café au Lait, Nutta, Envelopes and Pipe and another packet of pipe cleaners, quite a large parcel this time do you not think so Frank? I have an extra 1 lb tin of Café au Lait but I dare not enclose it this time as one is only allowed to send or rather not to exceed 7lbs in weight so I will send it in your next parcel. Do you know kid I have received five letters from you in two days, for all of them sweetheart many thanks, so up to the present, with the one exception No. 12, I have received all your other letters up to No. 55. I think I have been awfully lucky.

I am sending your old pipe mouthpiece just for you to see, no doubt you will remember it but I was rather amused when I went to the shop in the Haymarket to get the new mouthpiece. I said to the assistant man, 'I do not quite know as to the size of the mouthpiece' and he replied saying 'I should suggest a fairly thick one because he bites hard'. 'Yes', I thought to myself, 'I know all about that and his pipe is not the only thing he bites hard'.

My darling I am awfully glad you like your boots, I felt quite relieved when I got your letter saying they were a success.

You will have to forgive this short letter today sweetheart because I am anxious to get off your parcel without fail (I really ought to have sent it before this), and as it takes me some time to pack up even after the letter is finished, I am afraid if I wait to send you a real lengthy letter, someone, or a party may come in and prevent me from getting it finished. I went to Bedford yesterday, I did not go until the 12 train and the kid met me at a ¼ past 3 o'clock. We had tea together and I came home by the 6.10 train from Bedford. I did not think Bob was looking very well, not really, but she said she was quite alright, but she has a cough. In a letter I had from her about a week ago she complained about not hearing from you and said that in the future you would not be her sweetheart, but yesterday she was quite bucked, she had received a letter from you in the morning with the post cards enclosed so now of course all is well.

I much enjoyed going down to Bedford, the morning was wet and it rained when I was going to the station but the afternoon and evening were perfect.

Goodbye Frank dearest, I love you. I do not seem to have told you in this letter how much you mean to me, but you know because I have told you so often.

My darling, Frank.

Always your very own, Nell

Frank, my dearest one,

I posted a parcel to you kid on Wednesday but I do not suppose you will have received it by the time this reaches you. Re. your last letter that I got from you, No. 55, I was awfully amused where you speak of scrubbing your wee head with half a powder, I am so glad you found it quite good stuff and Frank dear, where you say 'At the present moment my tent has a scent which one of my youngsters says reminds him of Piccadilly on a warm night'. Shocking youth, how very dreadful, but at the same time I am quite sure I do not know what he means.

I am awfully glad your hair is looking quite nice, I believe my hair is in rather better condition now than it has been for some time, several people just lately have remarked on how nice it looks. I am dressing it in rather a different style, only a tiny bit different Frank, do you remember I had used to plait my hair in two plaits and then cross them over at the back of my neck, well dear now I do not plait the hair but take it right across at the back of my head quite plain and I still have the little curled bits just above but all my own hair, so when I meet you off the boat and we come up to Town to stay for at least two nights you will not be able to laugh at my extra curls. I had used to carry them in a small cardboard box, do you remember.

I am awfully glad I am using all my own hair, it is so much nicer. I really did want to change the style of my hair completely and I feel awfully inclined to do so now, only you have always said 'No, don't Nell' and I should hate to do it if I thought you would not like it so well as now.

My darling I shall not be able to seal this letter at least not with my ring, as I have left it at the jewellers in Bedford to be made smaller, it had worn so large and I got it rather badly caught in between two cases down in the cellar. No doubt the ring saved my finger but at the same time the ring was badly bent. I once knew a really nice man who promised to give me a signet ring. I really do not know how it never came about, do you remember? Tell me.

Frank sweetheart please advise me. I am rather hoping to give Bob a new bicycle for her birthday. Some time ago we sold her old one for £3.0.0. I am sending you several catalogues, I got them from Ruffetts and darling do you mind very much having a look through them and telling me quite at your earliest which bicycle you think would be the most suitable for her. I think there is rather a difficulty in the immediate delivery of the B.S.A. Bicycle, also the Royal Enfield so perhaps your decision had better lean toward the Rover. If I do decide to buy her one, I should like for it to be here quite by the time she arrives home for her holiday which I suppose will be about the first week in August, and do you think a 24 or 26 inch frame?

Of course I quite understand that just now it seems a lot of money to spend but Frank dear please do not think me extravagant. I have been thinking about her holiday which I suppose will be for about five weeks, I am quite sure I should not know what to do with her for all that length of time and she cannot go away for a holiday as there is nowhere for her to go, so it must be a bicycle, then she can get out and away from home occasionally. I feel sure you will understand.

I commenced this letter yesterday but I did not get it finished, you really would be amused but at the same time sorry for me if you knew the most awful difficulty I have some days in getting your letters off, dozens of times do I have to leave a letter before it is finished. My darling during the last few days the house and everything have been damnable, but I love you and just comfort myself that it can't be for very much longer. Goodbye sweetheart.

Your very own, Nell
P.S. Forgive me for troubling you about the bicycle but I really do not understand them, at least not very much.   Nell

22 May 1916   Number 42

Frank, my own darling,

If I had known those confounded Catalogues that I posted to you last
Saturday morning would cost ninepence for postage I should certainly
not have sent them, but no doubt I ought to have sent them in a different
way, leaving the ends open or something. I am posting you today two
newspapers, there is really nothing of importance in them but I thought
you might like to see them.

My darling, a week today and you will have been gone nine months,
does it seem so long as that to you Frank? In some ways to me it seems
years, but in other ways it hardly seems possible but of course I am
always busy and that I suppose accounts for some of the days going
quickly. I have just said I am always busy, but the Devil only knows
how I am going to manage this house through the Summer, single
handed.

We have had some topping days just lately, very hot but they do
take it out of me rather, although at the same time I just love the hot
weather. Yesterday, Sunday, I was awfully busy (please do not forget
the Asparagus which is rolling in quite a lot with the heat). Mrs Bonner
came in during the evening, she was looking so miserable and wearing
a very ugly blouse. I cannot for the life of me understand why Horace
Fletcher married her, I often sit and look at her and wonder what I shall
really look like when I get to be her age, but I do not know what that
is, she is always so tight about her age but I hope to God Frank I shall
never be so miserable as she, I shall not be, I have had by far too good a
time ever since I can remember that I shall always be able to look back
with pleasure on the days that have been. After I had tied up your papers,
I pushed in between a catalogue of Mr Marlow's sale. I don't quite know
why I did so but I thought it might interest you a wee baby bit, but of
course you remember him, he has been very ill and is still ill. I do not
quite know what is the matter with him but I think a nervous breakdown.
I think this was just a surplus sale to rid off some of the stock as he, like
all the farmers, finds labour very scarce.

Are you keeping quite well my sweetheart? I wanted a letter today
but I have not had one, it is a week tomorrow since I last heard from you

but I do not mind darling, I know I shall get them and of course I do not
blame you for the erratic way in which I receive your letters.
Goodbye my dear husband, please make haste and come home. I love you
just awfully, Frank, tonight.

Your wife-to-be, Nell

24 May 1916

Frank my darling,

Do you know really I ought to be attending to my finger nails [sic] instead
of writing to you, they are in a disgraceful state, and you would say so if
you could only see them. I believe this last fortnight I have rather given
them up as a bad job. I have such a lot of work to do and heaps and heaps
of things to attend to always that I just feel sometimes as if I can't be
bothered. Sweetheart I started this letter to you quite early this morning
and this is as far as I got. First of all some officer came in and then I had
lunch, since then two huge brake parties, the first this year thank God.
And yesterday the Engineers had another scheme on and four of the
officer men had rooms here last night so altogether I think it is charming
to be alive.

You must forgive me, Frank dear, for just grumbling a small bit in
this letter because I suppose I don't mean it, at least only a tiny bit of it.
I know where the difficulty is really, I am trying to manage this house
(and I am going to manage on my own or die in the attempt) but at the
same time I know it is just a tiny bit more than I can do comfortably,
and the result is I get rushed and bothered and then the whole thing
seems wrong.

Today is Saturday – I posted you a parcel Wednesday last. I am telling
you this dear because you may think it is a long time in between my
letters. Dear old Frank, I do want you to come home so that we can talk
things over. Ten months is such a long time, an awful long time when one
wants one as I want you. Frank sweetheart, wouldn't you have been
[un]happy if you had known on that last Saturday – I mean Sunday
night in August 1915 – that it was going to be at least 12 months before

you saw me again. I am jolly sure I should not have felt like facing the
time so perhaps it is as well that neither of us knew. I wonder when you
will be able to come home kid, I suppose you don't know. My darling,
I hope I get a letter from you tomorrow, it is nearly a week since I last
heard from you. I say a letter but I mean letters. Goodbye my husband-
to-be, I love you.

Always your very own, Nell.
P.S. Frank have you paid Hills? I received Bertie's account from there this
morning marked 'overdue' so when I feel very much like it I am sending it
onto Bertie with a very firm reminder.

26 May 1916   Number 43

Frank, my darling one,

Today is Friday and I posted to you Monday my last letter, No. 42, and
since then I have received five letters from you Frank, 'five darling'. I was
awfully pleased to get the last two letters this morning because I am not
well kid, don't get alarmed, it is only the usual that is happening, came
on yesterday the 25th. I shall be quite alright again in a day or two. In
the ordinary way I am feeling much better than I did a week or two
ago, perhaps I am getting fussy sweetheart. But to go back to your dear
delightful letters, thank you so much they have made me feel very happy
and once again I know that you do love me, of course I always know
that darling but just sometimes some of your letters make me feel rather
more sure.

   I have received the box containing your Winter underclothing etc.,
after being very carefully directed via Harlington it came through to
Dunstable but that was quite alright kid, I did not mind I got it from
there quite easily, if at any other time you are again sending I should
leave out the word Dunstable and address to Mrs MacVicar Armstrong,
Toddington, Beds. Via Harlington Midland. I think it is the word
Dunstable that is always so frightfully misleading on the parcels by rail.

   Right ho sweetheart, I note what you say in your No. 60 letter about
writing to you quite often, you are very preachy about it Frank but I will

forgive you, and as you know I do write to you quite a lot and I will keep on doing so because I love you and because you have promised one day to marry me, '<u>Some undertaking</u>'.

Your letter No. 57 about your spurs, what a nuisance Frank you having them stolen, of course dear I will try to get you another pair exactly like the last but it may be difficult now, anyway I will try to get you a pair of some sort and as nice as possible.

I love your tale about a fellow and a girl (neither of whom had been <u>too</u> good) got married, etc. etc. Thank you so much for all the tiny bits you pass on to me. Frank, my darling, in this letter you go on to say 'Nell darling, I want just awfully to be with you tonight, please feel a tiny bit sorry for me'. No kid, it is no good, I can't feel sorry for you, I have more than I can manage in feeling sorry for myself in that respect.

Your letter No. 58 where you speak about your boots again, I am awfully pleased they are a success because I was flunky about them. I believe I have told you before that when you ask me to get you anything you give me so little to work on, I mean dear no particulars, you just leave everything to me.

I think perhaps after all I will feel a tiny bit sorry for you because nine months is a long time. You tell me you have waited and my husband I believe you.

Always your very own, Nell

29 May 1916   Number 44

Frank, my own dearest one,

All is again well and I am feeling better. A fortnight today Whit Monday so I am jolly pleased to say I shall be quite alright then as things will not be happening until on or about today three weeks– June 19th. You are quite right Frank my darling where you say in one of your letters that I am not so strong as I try to make believe and especially just when the time is approaching I admit I do feel too beastly for words just then, is it not a nuisance but I have always been the same so by now I should have got quite used to it.

I am sending you Tobacco, Cigarettes and Spurs. I am not sure if the spurs are quite such a nice pair as the previous ones but tell me all about them in your next letter. I am also enclosing the two sets of straps as you did not say which sort you wished sent on. I have been struggling for about 10 minutes to find room in this box for the remaining tin of Café au Lait but without success, so next time with luck.

Sweetheart mine you will be sorry to hear that Mrs Bonner is suffering from Diphtheria and was taken to the Fever Hospital on Saturday morning last. I am pleased to say I had not seen anything of her for several days beforehand as Horace Fletcher has been home and she never or very seldom comes anywhere near me when he is here, I think she much dislikes for me to see them together, he was at home when the Doctor pronounced it Diphtheria so of course his leave is extended, I think they say for a fortnight.

The Diphtheria is really very bad in the village, fresh cases nearly every day. I felt rather merry when I heard about Mrs Bonner and felt jolly pleased I had not been in her company. I do not know what I should do kid if I got badly down with anything like that, but as I tell Rose, not under any circumstances shall I be taken to the Fever Hospital.

Dear old Frank, in one of your letters, No. 60, you say that very often you think of the house which is to be my home, and plan out all sorts of things you will have done for me. My husband, thank you so much for telling me, I too think of the time when I shall be married to you, I cannot quite picture our home, I wish I could, but I have never been able to do so. Last Saturday evening I was rather rushed and had to run upstairs for some change but even so I made time to just pick up your photograph (the full length one) from the shelf, and whisper Frank darling. I did then compare my Saturday evenings of now and the Saturday evenings I shall spend with you in the house that you speak of, our home Frank.

I loved you awfully, frightfully for just the few minutes I was upstairs. I was very so so, kid, as you know, but if you had only been there and willing, would you have been willing? It would have to have happened and the people would had to have waited for their change.

Fox tells me the Spurs are rather more in price than the first pair, but he does not quite know how much, but what I was going to say sweetheart is, as everything is getting dearer, do you think it would be wise to procure, tell me how many dozen French letters, because something will have to be done when you do come home if I feel then as I feel today.

I love you, not only love you but want you in that one particular way just awfully badly.
Goodbye my darling,

Your wife-to-be, Nell

30 May 1916   Number 45

My own darling one,

I am just going to write you a tiny wee letter today to thank you for your three letters received yesterday, letters numbered 61, 62 and 63. I was awfully pleased to get them, they cheer one up no end. Poor old Frank, so you too are rather rushed with work. I am frightfully sorry for you darling, it is quite alright having just enough to do but when one gets more than they can manage comfortably I think it is damnable. You say you will write to me just as often if you have to stay up all night to do it. It is awfully good of you Frank dear, but I shall understand if I do not hear from you quite so often.

My darling why I am sending you a wee letter today is that yesterday I sent you papers, and the day before, Monday 29th, a parcel with [a] long letter enclosed, but you may get this letter before either of the others reach you.

Alright sweetheart, about your boots. I will write to 'Kent & Costicks' about a second pair as soon as I get an opportunity, I hope I shall be able to make it quite clear to them by letter as I shall not be able to go down to Bedford, at least not for five or six weeks.

In my letter of May 29th I explained to you about Mrs Bonner having developed Diphtheria, so of course now it will be difficult for me to get away unless I leave Rose in charge. I should not be over particular about doing that, she has turned out to be a real good girl and I should be frightfully sorry if she thought of leaving me, but I think she is quite happy and contented. I want to just manage if I possibly can as I am doing now because I am quite sure that immediately you can, you will take me away. It will be a quick move all round when the War is over, thank God, the whole situation is impossible where Bertie and myself are concerned, but all the same I feel sure he will come home when the show is over, and not forgetting Tommy. I often wonder how we shall rearrange things but I could not be here with them both, and you away somewhere, could I? Please tell me.

My dear husband I love you and I do feel like you do and as you say, what a real topping night we should have if we were together.
Goodbye my darling.
With all my love,

Your wife-to-be, Nell

4 June 1916　　Number 46

Frank, my own darling,

Don't you wish you were here kid? I am all alone in the house. 5 o'clock, Rose has just gone out, I have been resting since 2.30 upstairs and have not been disturbed once. I suppose there are not many people out, really it is frightfully wet today and very cold, almost cold enough for a fire. Frank sweetheart that will be the time, our first Winter after we are married. I often think about it and wonder what it will be really like, I know I shall be awfully happy because I shall be with you, and you too will be happy, you must be, I shall make you happy, it will be my one idea in life to be always good to you and never once allow you to feel sorry for having married me. I was most depressed this morning but I think this Naval Battle has more or less put the wind up everyone. But this morning, even when I first got out of bed, I felt too fed up for words. Please forgive me for grumbling just a tiny bit, Frank, perhaps I ought to say a big bit, but I think on the whole I don't do too badly because you can understand and you do know what the damned monotony of this house is like, not overlooking the beastly crowd we get here.

I have just been reading your last letter, No. 63, again, and where you say 'If you do go away and keep your word about trying to look as nice as possible I fear the worst', and then you go on to say 'Because I know there will be some low brute running about after you'.

Why do you say low brute Frank? He might be some awfully nice boy, but there now Tommy spoke of you as a B. . . . r who had made London too hot for him. I have not heard again from Tommy but up to the present I have not replied to his last letter, the one sent from the hospital, but I ought to have done so, perhaps next week I shall get more time and be able just to write to him and say I feel sorry.

Referring again sweetheart to this letter of yours, you say, 'Dearest you shall never regret being so good to me and I swear that I will never as long as I live touch anyone else', Frank, and you mean it, they are no idle words are they my husband? You know what they mean? Never as long as I live touch anyone else. I have wanted many times for you to tell me this in your letters but you have never done so before, at least not in the same plain way. I don't know why I should believe you so absolutely, why I should put you as it were on a pedestal, because it seems to me the chief thing and to a great majority of men the one and only thing they live for, 'Women'. Tell me Frank dear, are the other of your officer men running straight? Or rather managing without, tell me? Where do they go to? I do trust you sweetheart and I cannot understand as to why at times [I am] feeling uneasy about you, I suppose it is only natural that I should think about these things because I love you so much. Just sometimes when I am doing my hair I pick up your photograph (the head and shoulders one) and if I could only explain to you, tell you just how much then I love you, how every tiny bit of me wants you. I wish I could tell you but on paper it is impossible.

My God Frank, before I knew you I had used to think how much I loved Tommy, but it was nothing like this.
Goodbye my darling, I want you, just you Frank, nobody else in the world, only you.

Your wife, Nell

7 June 1916   Number 47

Frank, my own dearest one,

Well, what do you think of it now kid? Are we not going from bad to
worse? First the Naval Battle which was very dreadful indeed owing to
the enormous loss of lives, and now Kitchener and his Staff. I suppose
there is no doubt about him being drowned or killed on board but this
morning's papers contain nothing more than the evening papers of
yesterday. I feel most frightfully sorry Frank, I have always been a great
admirer of Lord Kitchener, I think in a way I almost loved him. I suppose
somebody will take his place but I feel sure just now we could ill afford to
spare him.

I wished last night as I wish now that you were here just to talk to me
about it, but I always want you near me if I am anyways troubled, if it is
only the tiniest little thing that is bothering me. I did get a letter from you
this morning, No. 65, I was awfully pleased to get it because it is a week
since I last heard from you, eight days really, May 30th I received your
last letter.

Dear old Frank the Postman has just been, 3 o'clock, and brought
another letter from you, No. 64, the one containing the little sketch affair
of myself. I think it is really quite good kid, thanks so much for sending
it. Yes do, Frank, please struggle on until you have produced a full length
drawing and as you say without the chiffon drapery. I do remember all
the times I have said I can't do it if you look at me and I am jolly sure
I shall feel just the same again because it is nearly 10 months now since
I last saw you and it will be considerably longer than 10 months before
I see you again. I often think about it and I am quite sure I shall feel most
awfully strange when you do come back, just at first I mean, and over
these little matters.

Remember, you say, I should think I jolly well do remember, you were
always most persistent about it, even so I was satisfied and I do want the
time to come so that we can again be as we were then.

Yes I know what you mean where you say 'Just lately I have dreamt
about you an awful lot'. Poor kid, I am sorry for you and Frank dear, is it
not a damned shame when two people want each other as badly as we do

to have to wait on and on, but we have one consolation sweetheart, it will
be worth the waiting will it not? Tell me.
Goodbye my dearest of all men,

Your very own, Nell
P.S. When are you sending the photographs of yourself, I want them so
badly. Nell

9 June 1916   Number 48

Frank, my own darling,

Just one more tiny parcel kid, I wonder how many I have really sent you.
Some day when I get a lot of spare time I must count them up, quite a
number I am sure, but there now I always seem to be writing to you or
packing a parcel which I am sending to you. But ever since I have known
you, I seem to have done nothing else but just fuss after you, I love doing
so, I must do or am I jolly sure I should never have been able to have kept
it up all this long time.

Dearest I am most frightfully mixed up over the notepaper, I do not
remember if a short time ago you asked me to send you some but anyway
I am enclosing a pad of paper and one packet of envelopes with your
tobacco and cigarettes, and sweetheart when you reply to this letter tell
me if you have sufficient envelopes or would you like some more?

Bob is coming home this afternoon for half term. I am looking forward
to seeing her but at the same time sometimes when I am talking to her
I feel awkward and confused. Even in her letters she nearly always sends
her love to you and always asks after Bertie. I suppose in a way it is a
nice trait in her character, for years of course he was good to her and in
a way is now, and I suppose she can't quite understand it but I just feel
sometimes that she would not mention him, then I suppose if she didn't
it would denote her character as narrow and ungrateful. My darling,
I am afraid I have not made it quite clear as to what I mean but you will
understand and even if she does chatter a little bit about Bertie she is not
a bad kid, not really, and I am glad she is coming home today, we shall
have some fun.

After I got into bed last night I read again your No. 65 letter and went off to sleep feeling happy and most frightfully comforted. I love this letter Frank, especially where you say 'If you could stay on in the house until I have been home and can talk it over with you and made some arrangements for you'.

Thank you so much Frank my husband, and if you are spared to come back to me I know in the long run I shall be more than repaid for all the beastly business of waiting now.

Goodbye my darling, take great care of yourself for my sake. I love you so much Frank.

Always your very own, Nell

14 June 1916   Number 49

Frank, my own darling,

I have just been reading in the Daily Mail that in Salonica [sic] you are having it jolly hot, 90 deg in the shade. Note the date, June 14th, I am sitting writing this letter darling beside a huge fire and even so my fingers are quite cold, we are having beastly weather Frank, rain every day for the last fortnight and the whole of yesterday wet. I do not think it ceased raining for a tiny moment. The kid looked out of the window many times waiting for the sun but no luck. She was looking awfully well this time, quite happy. Everyone tells me what a fine girl she is, I think perhaps in a way she is but it makes me feel jolly old to have a great girl like her for one's own.

Frank dear I sent you a parcel last Thursday, I mean Friday the 9th, but by the time this reaches you if you have not received it you will think I am neglecting you frightfully but I am not kid, you know I am not. I love you by far too much.

And now sweetheart, about your No. 67 letter and the charming silhouette of your best girl. I was awfully amused when I first looked at it but really kid it is quite good, even the feet you have made to appear respectable. I hate the tiny bit of hair at the nape of the neck in both sketches but I will forgive you about this and what do you mean Sir when you say 'I am struggling with a much more risky drawing'. Frank you wicked wretch, I believe I know what you mean, when I first read your letter you may not believe me but I went quite hot and I am sure blushed a tiny bit. I wonder if I am right in my surmise of the drawing. If so, I should say it's all very well on paper but the real thing much preferred, by one who knows.

Anyway, sweetheart, if as you say it turns out pretty well I shall be just delighted to inspect your work and give you my very candid opinion.

Frank darling, I have no news, everything goes on in just the same old style. During the last fortnight I have been doing a tiny bit of gardening, I like to do it. It is a change but I really cannot spare the time, I find an awful lot to do kid, really.

In your last letter you say, 'stand in front of your glass just as you are and take a good look, then afterwards write and tell me how you think every tiny little bit looks, even to the squiggly toe'. No Frank, I am quite sure I can't and if you only knew how jolly cold it is here you would not be so unkind as to ask me to do so. I am sure that my squiggly toe is just as squiggly as ever, and the other parts of me I think about the same. One particular part I am sure of, it has not been disturbed since you left it, only with abundance of soap and water.

I must not write any more today. I have had a card from Kent & Costicks and I shall in all probability be sending you your boots this week. My dear husband, goodbye.

Your very own, Nell

17 June 1916   Number 50

Frank, my own darling,

Thank you so much for the three letters I got from you this morning, Nos. 68, 69 and 70. Enclosed in 69 your cheque for £15 and the tiny snapshots. I think the snapshots are delightful, the dear sweet puppies and their serious looking mother. I have looked at them already a number of times, I love puppies Frank, they are a great weakness of mine. The Lieut. Man does not look half bad either, what is his name? Do you like him?

I am awfully pleased you are sending me a tiny photograph of yourself, you say 'I shall have the proofs in two days time when they shall be sent to you'. Thank you so much sweetheart and Frank dear, if they do not arrive I shall be frightfully disappointed.

I am awfully sorry kid but I do not think I shall be able to send your boots and trees for probably another fortnight. At the present time there is a great difficulty in getting stuff, specially so if it has to be made. The trees that Kent & Gosticks sent to me on approval were from stock at 8/6d. I did not like them, I am quite sure you would not have thought them nice enough, immediately I opened the parcel and saw them I knew they were not quite it, so now Kent & Gosticks are having a pair hand made at 14/6d but of course dear it will mean a delay, but perhaps you are not really waiting for them, I hope you are not.

We have a sweet little robin's nest in the garden, tucked away, Frank, in some long grass at the foot of a plum tree. The kid found it first last Friday when there were four sweet eggs in it, but now there are four new robins. I go up every day to peep at them of course – I have promised to look after them – and when I write to her (the kid I mean) I have to tell her how they are going on.

My darling yesterday I posted you two Daily Mails with rather a peculiar case in them where an officer man of the 2nd King Edwards Horse was shot by a sergeant at Guiness's [sic] Brewery. Please darling when you reply to this letter give me your candid opinion about it, I do not know if you will be able to pass any opinion, as to me the whole thing appears to be very much hushed up.

Yes kid, I see by the papers things are on the move in Salonica [sic]. Frank, please tell me how is the word 'Salonica' pronounced?

My dearest one, a fortnight today and you will have been gone 10 months, what a jolly good job I did not know when you went away that it was going to be quite so long as that before seeing you again.

I have really been awfully brave about it Frank, don't you think so? But of course you have made it so much more comfortable for me, I mean in sending me a cheque every month. I have not been so worried about paying, hardly worried at all really. Thank you so much for the cheque received this morning, you are indeed good to me. I don't suppose I shall see you for at least another two months, making 12 months in

all, but I shall just go on loving you and waiting for the day when you
come back.

Goodbye my darling husband-to-be.

Always your very own, Nell

19 June 1916   Number 51

My darling, Frank,

Have you ever felt like Barney's Bull? I hope you have because that is just
how I feel this morning. During the last two or three days there has been
one God damned thing after another, but anyway, now for a letter to you
and I shall perhaps feel better.

I was delighted to get your letter No. 71, yesterday, Sunday (I am
awfully pleased when I receive a letter from you Sunday mornings) and
your little snapshot and a page from the Catalogue about Bob's cycle, for
all many thanks dear.

I have looked at the snapshot many times but there is something
about it which I can't quite explain, of course the breeches, puttee's and
everything are absolutely it, but perhaps it is the helmet that rather
covers you up, although I like you in it. I am jolly pleased to have this one
but at the same time I like where you say 'Another one will be ready in a
day or so, much better I hope. I'll send it on as soon as I get it'. Dear old
Frank, don't be frightened darling, I promise not to kill you when you do
come home because you say in your letter 'I am afraid you will kill me
outright, a glorious death kid but I don't want to die.' No, I don't want
you to die either, I shall want you to live for another day for just the same
purpose. I love where you say 'My longing for you is chronic'. Is it really
Frank sweetheart, do you want me awfully badly?

I often think about you kid in this particular one respect and feel sorry
for you but never mind darling, when you do come home my husband
I will be most awfully good to you. Referring again to your letter where
you say 'To hark back for a moment to your ring I somehow seem to
remember a fellow promising you another one but didn't he turn out to be
rather a rotter?'

Yes, you are quite right dear, he did. Do you know once, Frank, he took me to London, I was supposed to be going for 4 days and out of all that time I think I saw him for 4 hours, he was a beastly fellow.

You go on to say Frank, 'Tell me if you think he has earned, really earned your forgiveness'. Well, yes, I think perhaps he has, during the last 10 months he has been to me most generous, but even now at times I feel frightened and not quite sure when I think of spending any time [in] Town with him. Darling I will post you a parcel either tomorrow or Wednesday certain, so you will understand my dearest of all men should there be a delay in between this letter and my next.

Frank my darling I love you just awfully and as you say in your letter 'Stick it, however damned rotten things may be in Toddington'. Yes I will sweetheart, just for you. I would not, not under any other circumstances in the world.

Goodbye my darling,

Your wife-to-be, Nell

P.S. Frank dear thank you so much for the trouble you took over the Cycle Catalogues. I will take your advice.

26 June 1916   Number 54

Frank, my own darling,

I am afraid my letter that I sent to you Saturday was rather merry, if so I am sorry but we had 'Some' day here Saturday. I went to bed feeling most frightfully tired kid. In the early part of the evening I told Rose to keep a fire going as I should be using the bath, but honestly Frank I was too weary to even look into the Bath Room but I felt quite alright when I wakened on Sunday morning and fit enough '<u>for you</u>'. I was awfully pleased when Rose bought up my letters and amongst them one from you, No. 72. You say in this letter, 'If this epistle is even more uninteresting than usual please be kind and don't be very angry'. But Frank dear, I did not find it uninteresting and I was amused when reading about the pair of Scavenger Beetles and yes, I do remember the Wonder Zoo. I could just have stood and watched the Cranes for hours, the weird things how they jumped about, I do remember and, kid dear, the beastly creatures in the Circus place we went into. I forget what they were called, like men and monkeys. I've got it, but I shall have to get the dictionary to find out how it is spelt. 'Chimpanzees', I did not like them, even now when I think of them I feel creepy, and you go on to say 'What price the monkeys' disgusting creatures. I shall never forget them, never in my life before had I been so impressed. Personally I think there is no better game on earth for two people than love, but at the same time one does not want to advertise it in the way the monkeys did at the Wonder Zoo. I firmly believe you enjoyed watching them, Frank, did you? tell me.

Thank you so much my husband-to-be where you say in your letter 'Last night it was filthily hot and I could not sleep so I lay under my Mosquito net and thought about you'. I am so glad it made you happy thinking of the time when we are married. It will be lovely Frank, will it not? because as we have said so many times we love each other as few people do. Few people have had the glorious times together as we have. Do you remember how we have argued the point about you coming into the Bath Room, how you have just wanted to come in awfully badly and I have felt afraid to let you. Once or twice when you came in do you remember how you loved me, your hands just all over me and to think, Frank, there is going to be many nights like these.

I am just going to stand in front of you as long as ever you want me to and I shall try awfully hard always never to refuse you the actual thing. Tell me Frank, you would hate to be refused would you not? Do you remember the nights downstairs when I have just knelt down to you, you loved this particular way did you not? Please tell me.

I feel sure I proved to you by doing this my passionate love for you and I loved doing it. You say in your letter 'I don't think the woman lives who could make me forget for one minute I belong to you'. Thank you so much for telling me this, and all the lovely things you do tell me in your letters – they just help me to keep going, keep me living and writing just for you. Goodbye Frank my own darling boy, I love you.

Your wife-to-be, Nell

30 June 1916   Number 56

Frank, my darling one,

I really believe I have spoilt you, I am referring to your letter No. 75
which arrived yesterday in which you say, 'There has been a small mail
in today but I got nothing', then you go on to say 'I am a bit sick about
it old girl because I am so jolly anxious to hear that you are alright'. Of
course I am alright and you are getting into a real old 'grump ass'. You
just want me to write to you every day and I am jolly well not going to.
But seriously my sweetheart I am sorry there was no letter but I suppose
it is just the same with you, Frank, as with myself. I hate it some days
when there are no letters from you. I want a letter from you on every post
and you know dear it is just the same here as out there, at least for me the
same old weary monotonous thing day after day, heaps to do but all very
unexciting. My darling I like where you say 'I wish to God I could come
straight home and marry you Nell'. I too wish you could, just with all my
heart Frank I wish it, but you will not be able to for a long time, a year
from now at the very least, rotten luck I call it, having to wait when I love
you so much.

   Many thanks dearest for your other two letters, Nos. 73 and 74. I am
awfully pleased with the wee photographs and I think the one of yourself
first class. I shown [sic] it to Anderson last night, Flo Potts was here
she also saw it, we were much amused at Anderson because in the first
instance he had to hold it about a yard off to discern who it was, then he
wasn't quite sure, he thought it was Mr Armstrong, so when I told him it
was you he jolly soon handed it back to me with very little to say. I think
the silly old fool is frightfully jealous of you. I received a topping snapshot
from Bob last Sunday morning, taken at the baths, herself and two other
girls from the Howard College, it is really very pretty. I have written to
Bob asking her if she has another as I told her I wanted one for you, so
perhaps dear she may send one on to you, I am quite sure you would like
it Frank.

   Yes, I did see the Post Cards you sent to her but I forget the one
showing a typical 'Salon in Pub' and you say how would I like to have
customers like the old swine sitting outside. Sorry darling but I do not
remember the old chap in question, but surely, Frank, he can be no worse

than the majority of customers we get here. But when I go away from here there 'ain't' ever going to be any more customers ay darling? Tell me.

Dearest the enclosed I cut from Wednesday's Daily Mail, June 28th. My attention was drawn to it by Mr Kim Horley and I thought it might interest you but perhaps you know all about it.

Yesterday I posted you the Bystander and one or two papers. I really meant to take out a cutting from the Bystander, but somehow forgot so perhaps darling you will do so for me when it reaches you, you will find it in one of the back pages and it reads something like this, 'The effects of Uric Acid on the Hair'. If you find it send it along sweetheart as I want to write for one of these books. I also sent you a parcel Tuesday last, has it reached you?

Goodbye my darling, I love you and want you to come home to me. Ten months today since I last said goodbye to you. My God, what a long time Frank, don't you think so?

Your wife-to-be, Nell

1 July 1916   Number 57

Frank, my own darling,

I said in my letter to you yesterday that I jolly well would not write to you every day but I just feel, Frank dear, as if I want to write a tiny letter to you today because I love you and I am feeling frightfully lonely and I believe I feel a tiny bit like Mrs Chepstow in 'Bella Donna', just tired but she admitted to being 38 years but was really 42. I should think 42 is a ghastly age for a woman, supposing she has no one to love her. I should like to see the play 'Bella Donna' again. I wish you were at home so that you could take me. I saw it a long time ago with Tommy and the Sporting & Dramatic that I sent you recently reminded me again of it with Sir George Alexander and Mrs Patrick Campbell, did you notice them?

Frank dearest, this is just one of the days when I want you so badly to be near me, when I can think of nothing else, only you. I do have days like these when you strike me so much more forcibly than others.

To me it seems a long time since I first met you but at the same time it does not seem possible that it is three years. I believe it was on the first Sunday in June 1913, do you remember sweetheart quite plainly when you first saw me? Tell me please Frank. Since this particular day I have had some of the happiest times of my life and some of the unhappiest.

If I live to be very old I shall never forget when Bertie returned home from Canada after I had seen him and he came into my bedroom and attempted to make a fuss of me, if you remember I was and had been awfully poorly – you know what had been the matter don't you? tell me. But immediately I saw him I cannot explain on paper and neither could I tell you, but I knew that I should never want him again, never want his hands to touch me and as this feeling swept over me I knew it was you that had caused it.

I was in a dreadful state for two or three days, of course I knew even then you were fond of me but I was not so sure about you as I am now and I wondered what I ought to do to be right. After a day or two when I felt stronger I knew it did not want any thinking about and that if you did not want me, then it could never again be him. I remember at night time I used to lie in bed awake and I had used to think if you did not mean to marry me then I should go to Tommy. I knew at least he would be kind to me and understand.

But my darling the whole thing soon straightened itself out did it not? I shall perhaps make you tired by telling you this all over again but for the time being it was very dreadful for me and as I have said it left a lasting impression.

After we are married, kid, we shall have a lot of things to talk over. I wonder what we shall do with the kid when we are first married, she is already talking of finding something to do and in her last letter she asked me to advise her as what she would be able to do for a living later on. I did not know what to say in reply to this particular part of her letter so I left it unanswered but I too wonder, she is growing up so fast. My darling one goodbye,

Your wife-to-be, Nell

ᵠNDEX

Printed in Great Britain
by Amazon